FERRARI
308, 328, Mondial

Osprey AutoHistory

FERRARI
308, 328,
Mondial

GEOFF WILLOUGHBY

First published in 1982 by Osprey Publishing
59 Grosvenor Street, London W1X 9DA
First reprint 1984
Second reprint 1986
Revised edition 1988
Reprinted 1989

United States distribution by

Publishers & Wholesalers Inc.

Osceola, Wisconsin 54020, USA

British Library Cataloguing in Publication Data

Willoughby, Geoff
    Ferrari 308 and Mondial.—2nd ed.
    1. Ferrari automobile—History 2. Mondial
    automobile—History
    I. Title
    629.2′222   TL215.F47
ISBN 0-85045-832-3

Filmset and printed in England by
BAS Printers Limited, Over Wallop, Hampshire

Contents

Ferrari V8—
a true Ferrari engine

When speculation began about a possible successor to the well-established Dino 206/246 series of cars not many perhaps would have suggested that the engine to be used might be a V8. A survey of Ferrari's engines up to that time would have shown that no more than a handful of V8s had been used during the 30 years that the marque had been in existence; strong enough indication that such power plants were not in Ferrari's way of thinking.

But in the best part of fifty years in the motor industry, Ferrari the man, if not the marque, had had considerable experience of 8 cylinder engines. They had, of course, not all been vees, but whether of this configuration or of in-line type, they had furnished enough information on possible alternatives to the so-familiar V12s and V6s.

Just after the end of World War I, having failed to find employment with Fiat, Enzo Ferrari took a job with a man who was stripping the bodies from light trucks, reconditioning the chassis and then selling them to coachbuilders to be rebuilt as cars. Ferrari acted as both delivery man and test driver. It was in the latter capacity that he moved to the CMN firm in Milan and started to drive their cars in races.

In 1920 he joined Alfa Romeo as a member of their test department. It was from there that the

Scudieria Ferrari. Louis Chiron at the 1934 Monaco GP with one of the Scuderia's 2.6 straight eight P3 Alfa Romeos. The car finished 2nd in the race

works drew their race drivers. He was thus finally committed to the competition world, at a time when the face of racing car design was changing. Whilst eight cylinder engines were by no means a new proposition at the time he became active in racing, it is a fact that in the period leading up to the start of World War I the majority of races had been won by cars with four cylinder engines. When racing resumed after 1918 things became very different and with few exceptions racing became dominated by cars with in-line eight cylinder engines.

Alfa Romeo's involvement with such engines came with Vittorio Jano's design for their P2 GP car introduced in 1924. Thus Ferrari was in on the ground floor of 8 cylinder development insofar as

Type 815. One of the two cars built by Ferrari for the 1940 Mille Miglia. Their 1.5 litre straight eight ohv engines were based on Fiat 508C Balilla parts. One of the cars is still in existence

competition was concerned. By the time of the P3s introduction in 1932, when GP racing was officially recognised as having gone *formule libre*, Ferrari had formed his Scuderia Ferrari and was active in many forms of racing.

In spite of having gone to the trouble of designing a new car, Alfa Romeo were happy to turn over their representation in racing to the Scuderia. This situation prevailed until 1 January 1938 when the factory controlled *Alfa Corse* took over completely from the Scuderia Ferrari. Whilst Ferrari was retained to manage the new organisation, he did not find the loss of independence to his liking, and finally broke his association with the company in 1939.

During the time that the Scuderia had functioned, much of its racing had been done with the 8 cylinder P3 model. Also, with the freedom of action given him, Ferrari had undertaken development work aimed at keeping the cars competitive in the face of strong opposition. He had also been responsible for the design and construction of such cars as the *Bimotore* Alfa which used two 'P3' engines—one ahead of and one behind the driver—and involved with the superb straight eight, 1.5 litre Type 158 *Alfetta*. The latter, designed and built during 1937/38 was intended to participate in *voiturette* racing—the pre-war Formula 2—and made its debut in the voiturette race that preceded the 1938 Coppa Ciano at Livorno. When racing was resumed after the 1939/45 war, the Type 158 really came into its own, completely dominating GP racing during the period 1946 through to the end of 1951.

Thus Ferrari had gained much knowledge of 8 cylinder engines during a period when they had been in the forefront of racing, and the Type 158 *Alfetta* would become a classic long after he had left Alfa Romeo.

It is not surprising then that, when approached to build two cars for the 1940 Mille Miglia, he chose an in-line 8 cylinder engine for them, although that choice was suggested in part by the conditions governing the class in which the cars were to be entered.

These Type 815s as they were called, did not herald any serious interest in the 8 cylinder theme when in 1947 Ferrari emerged as a constructor in his own right. By then he had become chiefly interested in and concerned with V12 engines; not until 1955 would another 8 cylinder engine, this time a V8, become associated with his name. Curiously, it would be designed by Jano who had, 30 years previously, been instrumental in stimulating Ferrari's interest in eights.

Ferrari's first experience with V8s came about as a result of Lancia's ill fated Formula 1 venture during 1954 and 1955; the decline of his own fortunes in GP racing; the concern of the Automobile Club of Italy that Ferrari, and through him Italian motor racing, should survive; and the astuteness of Fiat in giving their backing to him.

Vincenzo Lancia had been a works driver for Fiat prior to the outbreak of World War I. From his experiences as a driver and his involvement in the financial aspects of Fiat, he had concluded that his own company should not become involved with racing.

When Vincenzo Lancia died in 1937 his son Gianni assumed control of the company. He was interested in motor sport and with the basis of a well organised technical team led by Jano, put Lancia cars into racing. From a modest start with sports cars, a GP single-seater, the V8 engined Type D50, was built, making its debut in the Spanish GP at the close of the 1954 season.

Unfortunately whilst the design was of great technical interest, the cars did not show up very

Inherited power. The Jano designed V8 engine in a Ferrari-Lancia Type 801 car at the 1957 Argentine GP

The 248SP saw another V8 in the rear of a sports-prototype, under the Dino name

well in the events they entered the following year. Also they had the misfortune to lose their Number One driver, Alberto Ascari, killed whilst testing a sports Ferrari having only days before survived an accident at Monaco which put both him and his Lancia into the sea. On top of that, financial problems came up, and Gianni Lancia lost control of the company.

Ferrari, having dominated GP racing in 1952 and 1953 since Alfa Romeo's withdrawal at the end of the 1951 season, began to go badly off form with the 2.5 litre fours designed by Aurelio Lampredi for the start of the new GP formula in 1954.

It was the poor showing of both Ferrari and Lancia that led Prince Caracciolo, then President of the ACI, to take action over the troubles besetting both constructors and the future of Italian motor sport. The latter, in repercussions that followed the disaster at Le Mans in 1955, was under attack from various quarters. Caracciolo suggested to Lancia that they entrust their GP cars to Ferrari. He also persuaded Vittorio Valletta, then President of Fiat, that the prestige of the Italian motor industry was at stake. The result was that at a handing-over ceremony at Turin in the courtyard of the Viale Caraglio on 25 July 1955, Ferrari acquired six Lancia D50s, supporting spares, documents, and the services of Vittorio Jano. Fiat also contributed to the deal by establishing an annual grant in aid equal to 50 million lire. That committment was to last for five years and could be taken in cash, components or technical assistance, including production time. One may speculate that this involvement was the first step on the long road that led to Fiat's ultimate controlling interest in Ferrari.

The new arrangements proved of immediate benefit. Under Ferrari's direction, a third Con-

In-house sophistication. Jano and Ferrari designed V8 in the 1964 Type 158 F1 car. Fuel injection came early to Ferrari racing cars

structors Championship and Drivers Championship were won by the marque in 1956.

However, this first involvement with V8s was not to last. The regulations governing Formula 1 racing changed again in 1958. From the results of tests carried out with his newly developed Formula 2 V6 Dinos, Ferrari had made up his mind that he would be using this configuration in GP racing.

Another brief flirtation with the V8 layout came in 1962. This time it appeared in a mid-engined sports car; one of a variety of machines which the factory and its customers would use in Sports and GT racing that year.

The new engine was first seen at the Ferrari press conference held on 24 February 1962. Reputedly it had been developed by Carlo Chiti from a study he had undertaken for a proposed '248GT' car. The Ferrari engine lists show that the engine for that was to have been a 90-degree V8, 77 × 66 mm, 2458 cc, with single ohc per bank a CR of 9.2:1 and an output of 190 bhp at 7500 rpm.

At the press showing two examples of the new sports car, the '248SP', were on view. Dimensionally the engine was unchanged from that of the projected GT car but the compression ratio had gone up to 9.8:1 and the power was quoted as 250 bhp at 7400 rpm.

The 248SP made its competition debut at Sebring. For political reasons Ferrari entrusted the entry of his cars to NART, the team run by his American importer Luigi Chinetti. The car driven by Buck Fulp and Peter Ryan finished a poor 13th overall and this rather dismal showing in its first race seems to have convinced the works that a few more cubic centimetres were needed. The bigger engined (Type 268SP) was available in time for the Targa Florio, run on 6 May. The additional capacity had been obtained via a new crankshaft which increased the stroke to 71 mm. The bore stayed at 77 mm giving the revised engine a capacity of 2644 cc. The CR remained the same but the power was now up to 260 bhp at 7500 rpm.

Of these two models only three examples seem to have been built. Their history lies beyond the scope of this book and the only certain item to be reported here is that factory involvement with them as works cars ceased in the year of their birth. For 1963 and subsequent years the V12 reigned supreme in Sports and GT racing. But not so in Formula 1.

The Jano designed V6 engined cars prepared for the 1958 GP regulations, brought Ferrari their fourth Drivers and Manufacturers World Championships that year. A 1.5 litre limit for unsupercharged cars was imposed by new regulations in 1961. To meet this, Chiti had designed a 120 degree V6 and with it further championship successes were gained in 1961. These V6s were not, however, truly competitive with their rivals, the V8 engined cars.

That lesson was not lost on Ferrari. He promptly set about the design of new cars to take over from the V6s. As a long term solution he favoured a reversion to 12 cylinders, but in the short term directed that work should be undertaken on a new V8.

Not quite ready for the closing races of the 1963 season, the first of the new V8 engined cars, the Type 158, began its competitive life in the Syracuse GP on 12 April 1964. The 90 degree twin ohc per bank engine with 64×57.8 mm bore and stroke, had a capacity of 1487 cc. Features were a five bearing crankshaft, aluminium-alloy crankcase/cylinder blocks, gear driven camshafts, one inlet and one exhaust valve per cylinder, and fuel-injection by Bosch. The CR was 10:1, and the output was listed as 205 bhp at 10,500 rpm.

Although for a part of the 1964 season the cars were not on top form, they picked up in the later races and brought Ferrari his fifth Manufacturers Championship and a sixth Drivers' Championship, John Surtees being the successful driver. The following year showed clearly that the design was not really up to mixing it with the opposition. Also, the longer term Flat-12 project was ready to come to the line. Running a mixture of both cars during 1965, Ferrari seems to have become convinced that for GP racing at least, 12 cylinders were needed. So, from 1966 onwards that has been the rule with first a reversion to the V12 layout, then, from 1969, a final acceptance of the Flat-12 solution. This prevailed until the emergence of the turbocharged V6.

Many people consider that the V12 engine is the truest expression of *Ferrarismo*. It is interesting to note therefore that up to 1973, the year in which, the 308GT4 was introduced two out of five Constructors' Championships and two out of the six Drivers' titles had been won with V8s.

CHAPTER 2

Bertone's turn— the 308GT4

An earlier book in this series has dealt with the Dino 206/246 GT cars launched in 1967 almost as a separate marque under the control of Ferrari. Whilst their origins are clear enough, Ferrari had never given a clear indication of the future he had in mind for this 'second string' range of cars.

Up to the mid-1960s, Ferrari's GT cars had developed for the most part along two broad but distinct lines. From a number of earlier models produced in very small quantities, some in 2+2 form, there was developed in 1960 the 3-litre V12 engined Type 250GT 2+2. Built on a 2.6 m wheelbase, it carried on into a production run that was Ferrari's biggest so far. All told, just over 900 examples were made during the three years that the model was catalogued. From that point on Ferrari have always listed a V12 front-engined 2+2. Succeeding models were the 4-litre Type 330GT in 1964, the 4.4-litre 365GT 2+2 in 1967, the 4-cam 365GT4 2+2 in 1972, the 4.8-litre Type 400, and currently the slightly larger capacity 4.9-litre Type 412. All of these were built for normal road use.

The second group of cars were the two-seater coupés and berlinettas which brought the firm considerable success in GT racing over a number of years. Most were dual purpose cars capable of road as well as track use. Their reputation was

The cover of this 1976 brochure shows the European version Dino 308GT4 as introduced at the 1973 Paris Salon. Note the restrained bumpers and button type side marker lights. The wheels are the same type as used with the Dino 246 series cars

established through the 3-litre 250GT series which, starting out on a 2600 mm wheelbase, subsequently found their best form with a shorter, 2.4 m wheelbase, model. In 1964 these were superseded by the 3.3-litre 275GTB. By then GT racing, as a result of changes in the regulations governing it and technical advances, had almost reached the point where it was no longer possible to race successfully a car that could also be comfortably used for normal road work. Henceforth GT cars would be designed for road use only, though there would still be room for those having a distinctly sporting image.

The Dinos were undeniably successful in bringing the Ferrari experience to a far larger clientele than ever before. If there was a flaw, it was perhaps that no attempt had been made to develop a 2 + 2 version.

The Modena-Bologna area houses, besides Ferrari, such constructors as Maserati, Lamborghini and De Tomaso. Ferrari was obviously very much aware of what his rivals were planning. Indeed, public notice of some of their lines of thought had already been served. At the Turin

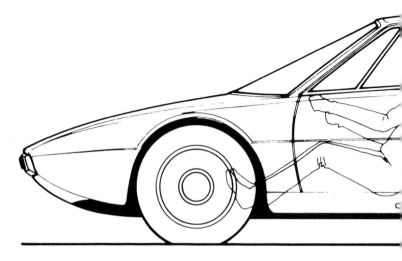

Show of 1970 Lamborghini had introduced the V8 engined Urraco and Maserati, at the Paris Salon a year later, had displayed their V6 engined Merak. Both cars provided a 2+2 seating arrangement. Further afield, Porsche had done just that from the word go—back in 1964 with their 911. Its large volume production, good sales record and continuing development showed that the concept of a 'small' high performance 2+2 GT had found favour.

If the Maserati and Lamborghini offerings caught the imagination, Ferrari could be losing sales to Italian competitors as well as the chance to take at least a part of the Porsche market. The decision, if taken, to introduce a 2+2 into the range would be logical if the Dinos were to continue as a separate marque. A measure of what was involved is given by Paolo Stanzani, the Director General of Lamborghini, writing in a special article for *Automobile Year* 1972/73: 'In my opinion, building a Gran Turismo car is the most complicated task in the whole field of motor car manufacture.

'What is a Gran Turismo car and what are its

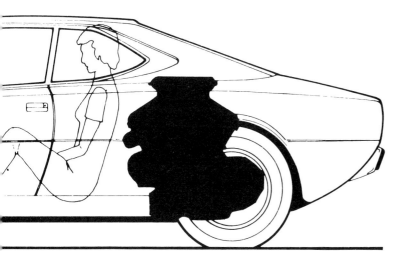

Styling optimism. An early Bertone sketch shows a roomy 2+2 arrangement. If seating were dimensionless, all would be perfect

essential qualities? It is a machine designed for use on the open road and, in addition to the qualities required for every other type of car, must also give outstanding performance. The ideal GT car should have the handiness and flexibility in city traffic of a utility car, the speed, acceleration, braking power and roadholding of a Formula 1 single seater, and be capable of transporting passengers and their luggage with all the comfort offered by a large limousine.

It should also be as handsome as the dream cars we admire at the Motor Shows'. The mix of qualities described, difficult enough to achieve within the scope offered by, for example, the 400 series Ferraris, Maserati Indy and Lamborghini Espada, becomes very much harder to get right with lesser versions.

Rumour, speculation and 'leaks' about a new Ferrari came to an end when the Dino 308GT4 was introduced at the 1973 Paris Salon, and it was then seen that Ferrari had decided to add a 2+2 to the Dino series. He had gone to Bertone rather than Pininfarina for the body and had chosen, for the first time in a production car, a twin cam V8 engine. In general layout there was no departure from that of the Dino 206/246 series. The engine/transmission/final drive unit lay across the chassis immediately behind the passenger compartment and ahead of the rear axle line. Fuel was carried in two tanks, one on either side, within the engine compartment. The radiator was mounted at the front. The main luggage carrying space was behind the engine and the spare wheel lived in a compartment at the front of the car.

With Lamborghini starting at 2.5 litres for their Urraco, and Maserati at 3 litres for the Merak, it had been fairly certain that Ferrari would have to go for something larger than 2.4 litres to keep their new 2+2 ahead of the opposition. Porsche had introduced a 2.4 litre engine into the 911 series in 1971 and comparative road tests of that car against the 2.4 litre Dino 246 showed that the German car was superior in some respects. As its designation indicated, Ferrari had gone to 3 litres for the latest car. This was a return to the engine size, that through the famed 250 series of V12s, had done more than anything to establish the reputation of the marque in the field of GT cars.

The reasons behind the choice of a V8 engine have never been stated. Certainly the V6 was nearing the end of its useful development, and a 2+2—being larger and heavier—would need more power to sustain, if not actually improve upon, existing performance. Also, regulations aimed at cleaning up exhaust emissions—which were becoming increasingly stringent—would make it difficult to obtain that extra power and still remain legal. There had also, on a number

Compact design. The engine of the 308GT4 resembled very closely that of the Dino 206/246 series. The carburettors lie in the vee with the gearbox/differential unit below and to the rear of the crankcase. The cover of the step-down gear train to the gearbox input is to the left

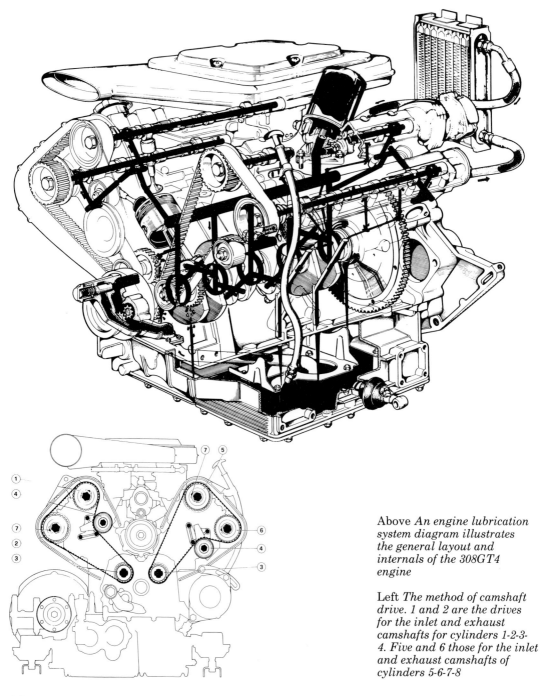

Above *An engine lubrication system diagram illustrates the general layout and internals of the 308GT4 engine*

Left *The method of camshaft drive. 1 and 2 are the drives for the inlet and exhaust camshafts for cylinders 1-2-3-4. Five and 6 those for the inlet and exhaust camshafts of cylinders 5-6-7-8*

of occasions, been some comment about the V6's lack of torque.

The Type F106 engine, introduced with the 308GT4, continued in use throughout the 308 and Mondial 8 series of cars until superseded by the Type F105 for the four-valves-per-cylinder 'Qv' and current 328s. A number of minor modifications were made to the original engine, for example at one time the method of lubrication was changed from wet sump to dry sump for some models. In line with a policy which ultimately affected all of their cars, Ferrari introduced fuel injection by the Bosch K Jetronic system on the V12-engined 400GT in mid-1979. It was carried over to the 308GTB/GTS cars in 1980. The chassis—apart from a special feature introduced for the Mondial range—and suspension have had very little modification throughout the whole of the 308 series of cars and have now been adopted for the 328s.

The description of the GT4 which follows is typical in its major details of the whole of the 308/Mondial/328 group of cars.

This engine view shows the single distributor per bank arrangement and the easily replaced single oil filter

The 90-degree V8 has a bore and stroke of 81 × 71 mm, giving it a capacity of 2926.9 cc. The compression ratio is 8.8:1 and the maximum power/torque output at the time of its introduction was given as 255 bhp/209 lb ft at 7700/5000 rpm. In meeting emission control regulations, figures as low as 205 bhp/195 lb ft at 6600/5000 rpm have been quoted for American specification cars.

The combined cylinder block and crankcase is a light alloy casting with the side walls of the crankcase extended well down in the interests of rigidity. Stepped cast-iron wet cylinder liners, a push fit in the block, are positioned for depth by flanges formed at their tops. These fit into counterbores machined in the block face and stand just proud of the block face when the liners are fully home. The water jackets surrounding each liner extend about halfway down their length. To limit block length, adjoining liners have mating flats machined on the flanges. The four throw crankshaft, machined from a steel forging, has five main bearings. The housings for these are formed in web partitions which impart additional strength to the crankcase.

Detachable alloy cylinder heads with hemispherical combustion chambers have cast iron valve seats inserted for the single 42 mm inlet and 36 mm exhaust valves per cylinder disposed at 46 degrees to each other. The valves, closed by double helical springs, are opened via bucket type tappets. Shimming is used for clearance adjustment. The inlet valves open at 34 degrees before TDC and close 46 degrees after BDC. The exhausts open 36 degrees before BDC and close 38 degrees after TDC. A single toothed belt per bank drives the twin cams on each head. The 308GT4 was the second of Ferrari's GT cars to make use of this system, the first being the 4.4 litre 365 Boxer.

Left *A good feature of 308GT4 instrumentation was the grouping together of essential information and a number of ancillary controls directly in front of the driver*

Below *This October 1973 photo shows more detail of the uncluttered and non-dramatic styling chosen by Bertone for the 308GT4. Much criticised at the time, it is now much more appreciated*

Below the engine, the crankcase is closed off by a box-like unit—the forward half acts as a sump for the engine oil, the rear forms a housing for the gearbox and limited slip type differential. A partition separates the different lubricants used. Engine lubrication is normally by the wet sump system but at one time for European versions of the 308GTB a dry sump has been used. A full flow filter is located in the vee of the engine on the left side and an oil radiator is situated in the left-hand rear of the engine compartment. Crankcase emission control ensures that oil vapour from the cylinder heads is drawn back into the engine through the air intake system.

In the cooling system, heated water from the engine is pumped forward by a single belt driven pump to the radiator and the cooled water flows back, via piping ducted through the centre of the chassis. A thermal switch operates two electric cooling fans mounted ahead of the radiator block

Four double choke Weber 40DCNF carburettors are mounted in the vee of the engine. Fuel is delivered to these by a single electric pump which draws from the left hand tank in the engine compartment. A transfer pipe connects that tank to the one on the right. The fuel is filtered between the tanks and the pump, and between the pump and the carburettors.

The ignition system as originally fitted had a distributor and coil for each bank with a single plug per cylinder. Each distributor had two sets of points. One retarded ignition during idling, the other, brought into operation by a micro-switch in the throttle linkage, operated during normal running. Later, a single distributor system was introduced but some cars—depending upon their destination—retained the original layout. Also, varying degrees of 'electronic' operation have been introduced. Firing order is 1–5–3–7–4–8–2–6.

A 9.5 in. diameter, dry, mechanically operated single plate clutch of the diaphragm type is employed. A stepdown train of three gears transfers the drive to the main shaft of the constant mesh 5-speed gearbox, ZF-type synchromesh being provided for each of the forward gears. The drive to the crown wheel of the limited slip type differential is taken from the centre of the second motion shaft in the gearbox. The gears are selected by remote control linkage passing beneath the engine. The drive to the rear wheels is by means of shafts with a constant velocity joint at each end.

The chassis, which is very strong and typical of Ferrari construction, has a rectangular central section built up of oval tubes. Fore and aft of this, square/rectangular section tubes are made up into frameworks, suitably cross braced, to carry the suspension and engine mountings.

The all-round independent suspension is by upper and lower fabricated steel wishbones, coil springs and double acting hydraulic shock absorbers. Anti-roll bars are fitted at each end. At the front the coil spring/shock absorber units are mounted diagonally within the wishbones. At the rear they are mounted above the upper wishbone to allow room for the drive shafts. All the suspension arms move on Teflon lined bushes. Steering is by Cam Gears rack and pinion.

Ventilated disc brakes—of 10.5 in. diameter front, and 10.9 in. rear—are fitted. Vacuum servo assisted, they are operated by dual hydraulic circuits through a tandem master cylinder. Fitted with 205/70 VR 14 Michelin XWX tyres, the $6\frac{1}{2}$ in. × 14 in. light alloy wheels were at first similar in appearance to those used with the Dino 246s. Later, the now well-known 'Pentastar' five spoke type were fitted as standard and 'wide' wheels ($7\frac{1}{2}$ in. × 14 in.) became available. The spare wheel is a $3\frac{1}{4}$ in. B × 18 space saver type.

At the front, pop-up twin headlight units—each with its own electric motor—retract into the body just ahead of the bonnet opening. Below and integral with the bumper are the direction indicator and parking lights. Lower still, in their own separate housings either side of the deep radiator air intake, are the fog lights which can be used for flashing when the headlights are lowered. On later production cars they were set in behind the protective grille of the radiator air intake when it was increased in width.

The interior trim offered was either full leather or a combination of leather and suede cloth. The latter material was reserved for the centres of seats and backrests, and for the backs of the map pockets in each door. The rear seats were obviously better suited to children rather than adults if anything other than a short journey was contemplated. Alternatively, they could be used to carry the sort of items that tend to enter the cockpit rather than the boot. An extension of this use was catered for by an option which replaced the seats with a luggage carrier arrangement.

The gate for the gear lever is mounted on the central console, along with switches for the electric windows and rear window de-mister; temperature and volume controls for the air conditioning; choke, ash tray and cigarette lighter and, if fitted, a radio. All necessary instruments come grouped together and clearly displayed in a binnacle directly ahead of the steering wheel. The end panels of the binnacle angle towards the driver. One end panel carries the heater controls. On the other are those for fog lights, hazard warning lights, and windscreen de-froster fan. The headlights and windscreen wipers are operated by stalks which protrude from the steering column housing.

The choice of Bertone as the stylist for the body has never been explained. From 1952/53 on, Pininfarina had been responsible for the design, although not necessarily the building, of the bodies for all GT Ferraris. Bertone had built one or two bodies in the early 1950s and likewise one or two 'specials' in the early 1960s. He had however been involved in the design and building of bodies for the 2+2 coupé versions of the Fiat's Dino. Towards the end of their production, Fiat had transferred the assembly line for them to the Ferrari works at Maranello. From the bodies delivered there, Ferrari gained up-to-date knowledge of Bertone's work. This connection, coupled with the reported full commitment of Pininfarina at the time has been cited as the reason for the

From above the separate luggage and engine compartment covers are clearly visible. Also the twin exhaust pipe per side arrangement. Note the 'Dino' script on the boot lid and the absence of any Ferrari horse

choice of Bertone. Others suggest that the decision was taken by Fiat following their takeover of Ferrari in 1969. Although designed by Bertone, the GT4 bodies were built by Scaglietti.

Relative to the exciting blend of curves devised by Pininfarina for the Dino 206/246 cars, the functional-wedge shape of Bertone's design made the 308GT4 seem, to some, a very plain car. More important perhaps was that it could easily be mistaken for one of its close rivals. Bertone in being asked to create a body for a 2+2 on a car whose wheelbase was only 8 in. longer than the 2-seater it was supplementing, had been given a very difficult task. With the passing of time a much more favourable and rational appraisal of the design has emerged.

Above *Never lift the lid on a Show special. The Rainbow's engine compartment shows some rather depressing looking steel tubing*

Above left *Pirelli P7s and Speedline wheels on the Rainbow*

Left *A matter of straight lines and angles Bertone's Rainbow at the Turin Show 1976. By no means everyone's cup of tea*

Bertone, probably stung by criticism of the conservative styling of the 308GT4, went to the 1976 Turin Show with a design that was exactly the opposite. The 308GT Rainbow showed that, freed from the restraints imposed by having to style a practical mid-engined 2+2, they could be as radical as the rest. The car, based on a 308GT4, chassis number 12788, but with 3.9 in. (100 mm) taken out of the wheelbase, is said to have derived its name from the unique fold-away Targa top which allowed rapid conversion from rain to sunshine use. When the driver wanted the top down, he had only to press a release button positioned in its leading edge. The pressure released the front and rear catches, and under movement of the driver's arm, the top moved back to a point where a system of hinges and counter-springs took it down behind the rear seats. To close it was simply a matter of reaching for the handle, lifting and pulling forward. It was a single-handed operation which *Car*, in their February 1978 write-up, assured readers could be undertaken at speed. They were able to do this because, unlike many other show specials, the Rainbow was a runner and had been driven for many miles on the road. A notable difference in its specification was the use of Pirelli P7 tyres, 205/50VR-15s at the front and 225/50VR-15s at the rear.

It has been said, relevant to the past, that no two Ferraris were ever completely alike. This was perhaps not surprising. Most of the earlier cars were made in small batches, anything from half a dozen up to twenty or thirty of a particular model. At times it seemed as if Ferrari had only to walk through the factory and see a pile of parts for a new car to be created on the spot. Now that production runs of several thousand cars for a type are not unusual, it might be expected that common build standards could be easily established, this unfortunately, (for ease of accounting) is not the case.

In common with other cars, Ferraris are subject to changes in specification, modification and variations in the options available at the time of purchase. Any modifications introduced, besides coming through in due course on new cars leaving the factory, may be mandatory or optional on cars already in dealers' hands and might possibly, at customer request for example, be applied to cars that have already been sold. The situation is further complicated by national homologation/type approval requirements which vary from time to time and from country to country. Some of these 'national' features can, as time goes by become part and parcel of all cars irrespective of their destination. Because of these factors, it is impossible to be precise about the details of either the specification or build of the cars throughout their production history.

When the GT4 came on to the American market, it encountered considerable sales resistance. In part this was attributed to Bertone's conservative styling, also to the use of the Dino name in its badging, and for the boot lid script giving the model designation. In an effort to overcome the problem, Ferrari issued a technical circular which gave details of several modifications that would be coming through on future production from the factory and could be carried out by the US dealers on existing cars. The Dino badges were to be replaced by those featuring Ferrari's prancing horse. Also, a chromium plated horse was to be placed alongside the rear number plate. Strangely no attempt was made to remove the 'Dino 308GT4' script from the bootlid and it continued to be used throughout the car's entire production run.

The ends of the exhaust pipes, which on the US cars had been curved to expel fumes downwards, were modified to suggest, by appearance, that they now discharged in the conventional manner. In fact they continued to operate as before.

The lower bodywork was painted matt black to give what has generally become known as the 'Boxer' look. A spoiler was added at the front below the radiator, and the front and rear energy absorbing bumpers, which had protruded very noticeably on the early USA versions, were replaced by a modified and less aggressive design. These changes add up to what are sometimes referred to as 'Series 2' cars.

Prior to and after these changes, American-market cars were easily identified by the large rectangular shaped direction indicator repeater lights on the sides of the body at front and rear.

Up until the advent of the Dino 206/246 series, road test reports on Ferraris had been few and far between. Most of the cars reported on had been loaned by private owners. Ferrari had no need to submit his cars for outside evaluation when the demand for them greatly exceeded the number being made.

As the Dino was to be made in a hitherto unprecedented quantity, and for a new market, it became imperative that Ferrari should turn to promotional methods as used by less prestigious makers. As a result, road tests began to appear in the motoring press on cars made available either through the concessionaire/dealer network or— less frequently than in the past private owners.

The reports published were either in the form of 'impressions' or full scale road tests which combined impressions with full test data. The value of such reports is often questioned and there are many variables that can affect the conclusions reached in them. Those that come from experienced testers or writers working for the technical motoring press should, however, be

able to give worthwhile clues to the characteristics and performance levels of the cars tested.

Paul Frère, writing for *Motor* was amongst the first to report on the GT4. He found 'an amazingly flexible and docile engine. This flexibility combined with the respectable output of 85 bhp per litre is perhaps the most remarkable and most endearing feature of the car. Not only is there not the slightest problem in using the car in heavy town traffic, but it makes life so easy on motorways where, after having had to slow down to 80 – 90 mph, all you have to do is to stay in fifth gear and push your right foot down to zoom past the car that got in your way. In fact the engine will pick up cleanly in fifth down from 1000 rpm (25 mph) and soar right up to the maximum speed of 152 mph without any flat spots or cam effects being felt.'

This was echoed by *Motor Sport*, in October 1974: 'Dino 246 drivers will gain two immediate

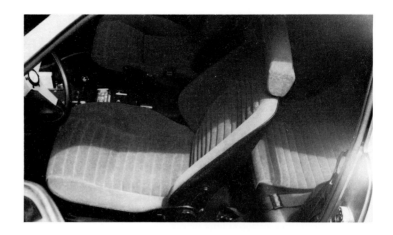

The leather with suede-cloth insert seats gave an air of luxury to the interior. All leather seating became available later as an option. The rear seats were not for other than short journey or occasional use by adults

impressions on transferring to a 308. First the good one: the torque and flexibility of the V8 is quite wonderful. On the one hand this impressive engine will rev to the definitive 7700 rpm red line on the Veglia tachometer, an utterly staggering number of revs for a road going production V8, and on the other it will crawl along and pick-up smoothly from just over 1000 rpm in fifth gear, equal to 22 – 25 mph. The torque curve peaks at 5000 rpm, but must be comparatively gentle in its shape all the way from 3500 rpm, for mid-range acceleration is excellent. Thus it is not essential to stir the gear lever incessantly for good performance in the manner one would have to do with the dynamo-like short stroke V6.'

The 'bad impression' noted was that the sound of the engine hardly did justice to a very high performance car costing, as it then did—£8000. Relative to the GTB/GTS models still to come, the GT4 exhaust note, whilst certainly different, cannot be said to have been noticeably out of keeping with the nature of the car.

Mel Nichols of *Car* magazine was equally enthusiastic: 'And what power there is in that engine. You expect performance in a Ferrari, but this V8 comes as a surprise because not only is it mail-fisted but its power is spread over an enormous rev range. There are no flat spots, not the slightest trace of camminess: the engine just gives more and more power as it revs. It is just like turning up a dial. The answer is the torque that just wasn't there in the V6—210 lb/ft at 5000 rpm compared with 166 lb/ft at 5500 rpm and all in a car that weighs only 250 lb more . . . An excellent device for city driving, whether blasting past slower cars into the gap you've spotted way up ahead, or simply for pottering in fifth as you talk with your passenger.'

Some may have felt on reading these reports of ease of pick-up from walking pace in top etc. that Ferrari were beginning to pander to the lazy driver. Perhaps they were to some extent. It was not altogether out of keeping with 2+2 concept that the driver should have an easier life, particularly in everyday traffic conditions where it was obviously expected that such Ferraris might now see more frequent use. Should it be needed, there was a decidedly sharp cutting edge to be exploited through more energetic use of the gears.

On the important subject of road holding Ferrari did not compromise. There were suggestions from some writers that towards the limits of performance, only the really experienced need apply.

Paul Frère noted: 'When cornering, the typical Ferrari understeer is evident but the faster you go, the less it becomes and there is a reassuring feeling of stability and safety in fast corners taken near the limit. Lifting off makes the car take a slightly tighter line, just as it should do, and straight line stability is perfect, the car also showing little sensitivity to side winds. Quick changes of direction are effected without fuss as you would expect with a low polar moment of inertia, but some of the inherent agility of this by no means very light car (it weighs 2930 lb with a full 17.5 gallon tank) is lost by the low-geared steering: the expert deplores it, but it may be just as well for the normal consumer.'

Mel Nichols, agreeing with much of what Frère had said, sounded a warning: 'Just as one expects a Ferrari to go hard, one also expects it to handle—especially if it is a mid-engined Ferrari. The Dino handles as easily as its engine performs: there is the characteristic touch of understeer, but the faster you go the more it is neutralised . . . but it (the steering) is fine for fast roads with sweeping bends. Along such roads, the Dino is sighted tight into the apex and then the power is squeezed on—hard. But therein may lay a trap for the unwary if they hark back too much to the old Dino. The V8 has such potency that power oversteer is very readily available; it can be induced in a way that it never could in the V6. It can come unintentionally until you realise the extent of the power reaching the rear wheels in second or third gears. This may not be so good for those who buy Ferraris for the name rather than the pleasure; for those who buy the cars to drive, it is excellent.'

Autocar testers noted another characteristic: 'Provoked further, the front wheels begin to understeer until ultimately full lock poses the limitation. However, it is necessary to exercise great caution in lifting off the accelerator in mid-corner since the transition to power-off neutral or oversteer condition is very sudden. On wet roads it was found to be most difficult to sustain a full power drift once the initial understeer had been "killed" by lifting off and indeed once any degree of power oversteer had been set up, sudden lifting off would cause the car to spin.' They conceded though: 'However, these are circumstances

The owner of this 308GT4
has put the 'Dino' script
below the licence plate and
'Ferrari' on the boot lid

which one is most unlikely to repeat on the road
and when driven at any speeds short of the
absolute, the Dino has a go-where-you-point-it
accuracy that is most reassuring.'

Doug Blain, also of *Car*, put the case in rather
more detail: 'It (the 308) has more to give in the
way of performance, ride and roadholding, than
ordinary mortals nurtured on the limitations of
mass production and computerised development
have any right to expect. It does reach out and
meet you half way when the moment comes to
take the wheel, so that there is no mystery about
extracting from it at least nine-tenths of its
performance potential—a pretty good rule of
thumb.

'My only reservations, I suppose, concern the
remaining 10 per cent, and it is in this area that I
always feel drawn towards the philosophy of
Lamborghini rather than any of the others. For
the Dino 308 is not really a forgiving car. As I
started to explain earlier, its limits of adhesion are

extremely high, and in ideal conditions its handling is such as to allow one to explore them quite comfortably. However, at the very point I mentioned where the car's natural rearward weight bias finally conquers all the initial understeer and the long, beautifully balanced neutral period which the designers and development engineers have superimposed by the use of every possible kind of cleverness, there is a grey area in which only the very experienced will feel at home. As soon as the conditions become tricky, this characteristic is of course exaggerated.

'During part of my time with the car, it was raining quite hard. This is such a rare event in Italy in the summer, and so relevant to the sort of conditions we are bound to encounter in this country, that I was determined to take maximum advantage of it. I spent the whole two or three hours of that rainstorm belting up and down the side of a miniature mountain that happened to be handy, gaining confidence with every transit and getting correspondingly bolder in the bends. Finally, after working myself up into a nice little sweat like they do at the races, I reckoned I was just about getting the best out of the car—only to find I was enjoying it a good deal less than earlier on.

'For the Dino is not the sort of sports car in which you hang the tail out for fun. Towards the edge of its adhesion graph one is battling a bit at the wheel, fighting off the oversteer which threatens to take over on every bump and with every unexpected tightening of a turn, prodding it back again in an effort to counteract the frantic understeer caused by an unsuspected puddle or loose patch ... and when occasionally the tail does fly out, it's essential to move with lightning rapidity to get it back in line.'

Obviously, in extending the 2+2 concept to the

Dino range, Ferrari had not cast it fully into the mould of the larger versions. The appeal to the more sporting type of driver still lay high on the list of priorities and it must have been accepted that the '+2' aspect was more in the spirit than the practice.

The subject of steering brought forth a mixed bag of comments. Some critics felt that it was on the heavy side at low speeds, others that it wasn't. Whatever the truth about that aspect of its use, there was general acceptance that as speed increased, it lightened considerably and posed no problems. Criticised was the $3\frac{1}{4}$ turn lock-to-lock and turning circle of 39 ft—it remains much the same on the latest in the line, the Mondial 8.

Braking was well up to the standard for the class of car. Only the American *Road Test* commenting that on the road the brakes had seemed powerful and well balanced, queried whether 'the difference between carefully modulated racing stops and panic stops had been programmed into the Ferrari computer'. Their panic stops—and they considered that in such instances drivers simply trod straight on the brake—had produced some locking and lurching that they were not entirely happy about.

Ride aroused generally favourable comment. Frère was of the opinion that apart from the characteristics of the engine: 'perhaps the most outstanding feature of the 308 is the excellent ride it provides'. There was no low speed harshness and at speed the irregularities of the road were smoothly damped out. Mel Nichols commented in almost the same vein. *Autocar* were not so enamoured of it at lower speeds. They felt that limited wheel travel and fairly stiff springing gave a poor low speed ride. They conceded that as speed increased, things improved considerably.

There were some adverse comments about the

Gone are the days. 'Mass' production has become the order of things. 308GT4 engines awaiting installation. Part of the car production line is in the background

level of engine noise inside the cockpit. Paul
Frère thought it was certainly worth directing
some attention toward a cure in the course of
development. *Autocar* rated it better than average. The *Road Test* was quite definite ' . . . inside
the cockpit the noise level is something only a
Ferrari freak could love. At 70 mph our noise
meter shook around the 81 dBA mark, and at full
throttle in first gear it reached 93.' The latter was
perhaps a rather academic exercise. *Road &
Track* in their September 1975 issue carried a
comparative test of the GT4, the Lamborghini
Urraco and Maserati Merak. From their noise
measurements the Ferrari was generally up a few
points on the scale compared to its rivals.

Generally criticized were the heaviness of the
clutch and the necessity to floor the pedal in order
to change gear—no great problem on the open

road but wearying in town. One report questioned the wisdom of using a diaphragm type
clutch with its tendency for the clutch pedal to
stay down as the operating mechanism went over
centre at high speed, but it seems that such
occasions were few and far between.

On the '+2' aspect of seating, most agreed that
it was really intended more for children than
adults, and young children at that.

Most were restrained in their enthusiasm for
the styling of the body. It was left to Jonathan
Thompson in his review of styling for *Road &
Track's* comparison report noted above, to say:
'The Bertone designed 308 is the newest design,
having made its debut in the fall of 1973. Hardly
anyone, not even the most loyal Ferrari en-
thusiast was much impressed by the first photos of
the car, but a close up inspection reveals many

*This photograph taken at the
factory in 1979 shows a later
version of the 308GT4. The
front bumper has been
changed and the grille
extended across the full
width of the car. The 'Dino'
badge has been replaced by
that of 'Ferrari'*

virtues. It's a design that grows in appeal with familiarity and which will have a greater influence on future mid-engined cars than the Merak or Urraco. Bertone worked very closely with Ferrari engineers to solve some of the visibility and engine access problems associated with the mid-engine configuration and its body is the most functional and honest.' There is no doubt that almost ten years afters its debut, the GT4 is by no means out of place alongside contemporaries in matters of styling.

Insofar as performance figures covering acceleration etc. are concerned, there are several sets of these—all different—available from reports in English language journals. The following table gives in brackets a spread of data from a number of tests set against *Autocar's* report of 13 March 1976. The 'as tested' weight of the car on that occasion was 3290 lb.

mph	sec	mph	sec
0–30	2.5 (2.2/2.7)	0–80	11.4 (10.5/12.3)
0–40	3.6 (3.6/4.6)	0–90	15.2
0–50	5.4 (5.1/6.0)	0–100	18.1 (16.5/18.1)
0–60	6.9 (6.9/7.7)	0–110	22.4
0–70	9.1 (9.1/9.7)	0–120	30.3 (24.6/30.3)

Autocar also gave figures for acceleration in the top three gears.

mph	Top	4th	3rd	mph	Top	4th	3rd
20–40		6.1	3.7	80–100	8.7	5.7	
30–50	8.4	5.1	3.4	90–110	10.5	8.0	
40–60	7.9	4.9	3.4	100–120	13.0		
50–70	7.6	5.1	3.7				
70–90	8.0	5.7					

From that test the following figures are quoted: Standing quarter miles, 14.9 sec/89 mph: standing kilometre, 27.6 sec/117 mph. Maximum speeds in

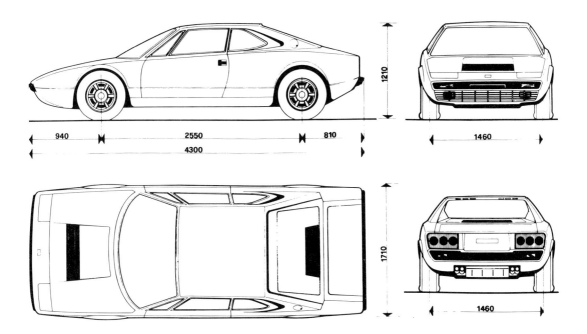

gears, 1st/45 mph, 2nd/64 mph, 3rd/90 mph, 4th/123 mph, 5th/154 mph. Fuel consumption, overall mpg—19.8. Hard driving, difficult conditions—17.8 mpg; average driving, average conditions—21.9 mpg; gentle driving, easy conditions—25.7 mpg. These figures for fuel consumption can be compared with more recent ones resulting from the Department of Transport tests of, urban cycle—12.2 mpg; constant 56 mph—22.3 mpg and constant 75 mph—19.2 mpg. In general then, the GT4 had been given a good press. With its wider appeal and once the initial reservations about its shape had been overcome, there was little doubt that it would find a ready market. If at the time of its introduction the intention had been to carry on with the Dino marque, it was the logical extension of the series. But as the decision was made to drop the Dino label, it became an excellent base car for the 308 series.

Principal dimensions—in millimetres—of the 308GT4

45

By way of summing up at this point, *Road Test* made an interesting judgement in their March 1976 report on the car. 'Ferrari is unique in all the world. Maserati builds engines for Citroëns and machine tools. Lamborghini got started building tractors. But Ferrari builds racing cars and high performance sports and touring cars, and nothing else. Ferrari is as much a legend as it is a real company; there is substance and there is myth and it is difficult to discern where one ends and the other begins.

Looking back, comparing past Ferraris with the newest one, this Dino 308GT4, it is apparent that Ferraris have never been really modern cars. It is surprising that we never seemed to notice it before: perhaps we were just mesmerized by the name and the sound. Think about it. Long after other major sportscars were built with space frames or monocoque unit bodies, Ferraris were still sitting on large-tube ladder frames. Ferrari was one of the last holdouts of the live rear axle among the higher performance automobiles. It continued to build large front-engined cars when Lamborghini was building the Miura and Maserati the Bora.

The Dino fits into the pattern. The structure is a space frame, constructed of square tubing with what looks to be a plethora of hand welds. And, even with the modern systems available, it continues to use four carburettors instead of fuel injection. The Dino is not a modern car. It is a 'current' version of a Ferrari and thus, most importantly, fulfills the function of being a Ferrari more than it fulfills the function of a modern, fast automobile. It is conceptually the same as all Ferraris and stands today simply as an extension of the mystique.

Pininfarina again with the 308GTB

The 308GT4 had, with its 3-litre V8 engine, indicated the sort of car that might eventually take over from the Dino 246 series. The latter had been in production for the best part of four years and that was about the limit for any Ferrari.

Those who had regarded the GT4 as something of an interim aberration, and were anxious to see what the real successor to the Dino 246 would be like, had to wait until September 1975 for the first public announcement of the 308GTB. There had, of course, been the usual 'revelations' prior to that time. *Road & Track* for example, in their June 1975 issue had come up with what proved to be a remarkably accurate set of sketches of the new car by Mark Stehrenberger. Following closely upon the September announcement, the car was officially introduced in October at the Paris Salon. Under the skin obviously a direct descendant of the GT4, its badges and associated brochures nevertheless made it quite plain that it was to be regarded as a Ferrari, the first non-12 cylinder GT from the marque to bear the name. Any pretence at a continuation of the marque Dino was gone.

The faithful were pleased to see a reversion to Pininfarina's for styling the bodies that would be built by Scaglietti and made of fibreglass. It was the first time that the bodyshell of a production

*Top Paris Show 1975. The
308GTB makes its debut.
There is general acclaim for
the Pininfarina designed
body*

*Bottom Paris Show 1975.
Three-quarter rear view
reveals the single exhaust
pipe on the left of the car.
Some complain that it now
hardly sounds like a Ferrari*

Ferrari had been made entirely of that material. Aluminium was used for the cover over the front stowage. Reputedly Ferrari, anxious to get the new car into production, had chosen it because it was quicker to produce the moulds for fibreglass than to make dies for steel pressings. There was in addition the promise of lighter weight and a definite advantage in the absence of a rust problem. Whatever the true reasons for its

selection, the exterior finish of the new bodies was very highly rated by all who examined them. Almost from the start it was doubtful whether the use of fibreglass would be anything more than a stop-gap or perhaps an experiment. Information, later proved correct, was that the next model in the series would revert to steel. In the absence of any authoritative explanation of this change of heart, a number of possible reasons can be surmised. It might have been that fibreglass had only been used because at the time it had allowed an earlier introduction of the GTB. Other reasons put forward have been that the fibreglass bodies were more time consuming to make than had been envisaged, their production subsequently fell behind demand and also that it was very difficult to find adequate repair facilities. By approximately mid-1977, steel once again reigned supreme, albeit tempered with selective use of fibreglass.

Insofar as styling was concerned, Pininfarina had instilled some of the old magic by skilfully blending together elements from the Dino 206/246 series and from the 365GT4 BB—the Berlinetta Boxer. The latter had provided the double bodyshell appearance resulting from the groove cut into the body at bumper level, the plunging nose and the rather square rear with sail panels extending back to meet a shallow spoiler. From the Dinos came the recessed concave rear window and unmistakably, the conical air intakes scooped out of the sides of the body just ahead of the rear wheel arches. The one on the left is for the oil cooler, the right-hand one leads to the air cleaner.

The engine/transmission unit remained basically that of the GT4 but there were some odd goings on with the lubrication system. While European versions used dry sump, those for the American market retained the wet sump arrange-

Top *Brochure centre spread illustrates the principal features of the new car's layout which remains very much that of the 308GT4*

Right *Peter Coltrin's camera has caught a 308GTB at the Fiorano test track*

Below right *Factory test car*

Below left *Engine cover is a mass of metal requiring delicate closing*

ment of the GT4. Quite why this shoud have been so has never been explained. It is possible that the engine compartments of the American cars, which were becoming more than a little cluttered with anti-smog equipment, could not cope with the added complications of dry sump lubrication. In addition to the normal crankcase emission control, fitted irrespective of a car's destination, the US models were equipped with air injection into the exhaust ports, and the means of preventing the release of fuel vapour into the atmosphere. The former called for the installation of two air pumps together with associated valves and piping, and the latter for more pipework, valves, a carbon trap and a liquid vapour separator. The value of dry sump lubrication on a car like the GTB—designed more as a sports car than as high speed transport—was underlined when *Road & Track* abandoned their skidpan testing because of zeroing oil pressure. The chassis followed very closely that of the 2+2, but with only two people to be carried, the wheelbase was shortened by some 21 cm to 2340 mm—the same as for the Dino 246. Front and rear track dimensions were unchanged from those of the GT4. Overall width

Below left Cockpit shot shows that some of the instruments and controls have been removed from the driver's direct vision. The clock and oil temperature gauge have been placed below the fascia. The switches on the door rest allow the driver to control both sets of electric windows

Below right The engine compartment of the 308GTB is practically identical to that of the 308GT4. A single distributor has become standard on European cars

was slightly less, and overall length shorter by 70 mm.

The final drive and first four ratios in the gearbox were identical to those of the GT4 but fifth was slightly higher—0.918 compared with 0.952—to give a few less engine revs when cruising.

A number of changes were made in the cockpit. The standard interior trim was leather with no option. Most of the instruments were placed in a tall binnacle jutting up from the fascia. The oil temperature gauge and an electric clock were separate, tucked away below the fascia on the driver's side. The heater/air distribution controls were moved to the central console, and the switches operating the electric windows taken out to the tops of the rather elegant arm rests which curved down the interiors of the doors in continuation of the fascia. The driver could control both windows, the passenger that on his side only.

At the front of the car the retractable headlight pods now housed single light units which combined main and dipped beams. The louvres behind them dispersed hot air from the radiator. Below, as on the GT4, were the direction and parking lights, no fog lights were fitted. At the rear the lighting layout had changed from the single, rather rectangular covers on each side, to twin circular units. Of these, the outer ones were the direction indicators and the inners combined parking/stop lights with central reflectors. It would seem that only the European versions had reversing lights—one either side—located in the rear bumpers.

The US cars retained the GT4's quadruple exhaust pipes (two each side) leaving the European models to discharge through a single outlet on the left of the car.

Above *Typical local countryside around Maranello. Ancient and modern influences*

Left *There is now a one-piece lid over the engine and luggage compartments. The contents of the latter are protected by a zip round soft cover*

Right *The single outlet exhaust layout shows up well in this photo*

Right *Official Ferrari photograph to cover the UK introduction of the GTB at the 1975 Motor Show*

Below *308GTB, US version. This rear view shows the changed position of the parking/stop and indicator lights; the plain with no reversing lights bumper and the twin pipes per side exhaust*

The standard wheel size was $6\frac{1}{2} \times 14$ in. front and rear with Michelin 205/70 VR14 XWX tyres. $7\frac{1}{2} \times 14$ in. rims were optional and seemingly soon became 'standard' on cars entering America. Whilst the Americans carried a full size spare, the Europeans continued to be supplied with the narrow section 'get-you-to-the-nearest-garage' type.

Behind the cockpit the separate covers over the engine compartment and boot were replaced by a single cover hinged at the front.

In line with the Dino 246 series, it was almost certain that a spider version of the 308 would be the next model. It would also be in keeping with a Ferrari tradition dating back to at least the early 1960s, of providing an open car to supplement the closed berlinetta and coupé models. Those interested in fresh air motoring were kept waiting until the Frankfurt Show in the autumn of 1977 before the 308GTS was introduced.

The body, from Pininfarina—to be built by Scaglietti—followed the principle adopted for the 246GTS of retaining as closely as possible the styling of the closed car, and providing a removable Targa type roof.

In line with late 1976 GTB production, the GTS bodies were a composite of steel—the principal material—aluminium and fibreglass. The floor-pan, removable roof panel and lower parts of the body were of fibreglass, the cover over the front stowage space aluminium and everything else steel.

The rear quarter lights, retained with the revised roof layout, were covered with louvred panels reminiscent of the sail panels on the early 1957 versions of the 250 series Tour de France berlinettas. In this latest application they were strictly a styling gimmick which needlessly restricted the driver's vision to the rear quarter. Both were hinged at the front and lockable. That on the left concealed the fuel filler cap. On the right it was merely openable to allow the glass to be cleaned. The detachable roof panel was easily removed for stowage behind the seats within a vinyl waterproof cover.

Road & Track in their July 1978 report on the car noted that the open top map pockets on the door interiors had given way to a closed latched type seemingly replacing the small lockable glove box in the central console.

Right *For a* Road & Track *report by Bob Bondurant this 308GTB was fitted with 225/60VR15 Pirelli P7s on 15 × 9.5-in BBS wheels from Intermag*

Another notable feature of that car, and of the one reported on by *Car & Driver* in the same month, was that the engine cover louvres had been extended further back and for the last five or so rows, ran the full width of the cover.

Mechanically, with one notable exception, the spiders were for all intents and purposes identical to the GTBs. The exception was that irrespective of destination, wet sump lubrication was used.

In the road test reports of these two models, most of which concentrate on the GTB, Pininfarina has been applauded for getting the styling back on to what are generally considered to be the right lines. Without doubt, most testers were happier with the performance of the two seaters.

Mel Nichols in the July 1976 issue of *Car* praised the way the GTB behaved at speed on the autostrada: 'I rejoined the motorway from Bologna back to Modena and after watching a Daytona closing steadily on me as I sat on a relaxed 130 mph and then seeing him disappear into the distance at something well in excess of 160 mph with no apparent concern on the face I saw in his mirror, I opened the GTB right up. It answers like the thoroughbred that it is. It surges forward with spirit, the tachometer and speedom-

Below left *The optional deeper front spoiler is visible on this 308GTB being got ready for exhibition in Germany by Auto Becker, Ferrari's West German importer*

Below *Unless crashed it's difficult to distinguish a fibreglass shell from a steel. Here's fibreglass*

eter needles climbing in unison, and the sound behind your head growing more and more intense, until there is just no more to come. In fact, the speedo was reading just over 160 mph, but the tachometer said it was incorrect. At this speed, like the GT4, the 308GTB is outstandingly stable. It moves not an inch from the path you have selected, goes unmolested by crosswinds and sits down on the road with a security you can feel through your backside. It's a *good* feeling.

'So too is the feeling of sheer security imparted by the car when it is flat-out through a bend or being thundered through a dip, as it was for mile after mile on the way from Maranello south through the mountains, down the other side towards Florence, and then back again along that magnificent driving road called the Passo della Futa.'

Paul Frère reporting for *Motor* in November 1975 noted that at speed on the autostrada the car had felt utterly stable. *Autocar* on the other hand, in their 23 October 1976 issue, said that in measuring the maximum speed—some 154 mph— it had only been attainable in quite still air as the slightest cross wind led to very disconcerting weaving at speeds in excess of 130 mph. They give a possible reason for this by saying that their run was made with sufficient load in the boot to bring the nose up. It is interesting to note that a deeper front spoiler was later available as an option.

Nichols (incidentally he was still calling the car by its discarded name) had a chance to put the car through its paces on some of Italy's more demanding mountain roads: 'The Dino comes so smoothly, so effortlessly into the bends. It has more of a softness about it than the 308/GT4, a gentleness; even more poise. There is a manifest feeling of sweetness, and you tend to trust it

Below right *Identification at an early stage. 308GTB body shell is tagged for identification before going on to final assembly*

Below *Destined for the UK this rhd GTB has the deep front spoiler and wheels fitted with Pirelli P7 tyres*

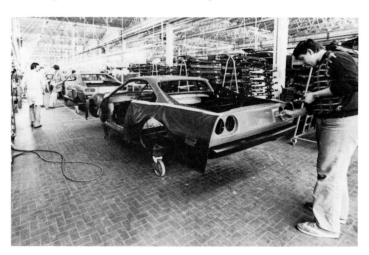

308GTS on display with 308GT4 behind it and 400 in front

implicity from the outset for you can sense how outstandingly well-balanced it is. You begin to go faster, unable to resist that track with its corners from the world's Grand Prix circuits. There is a gentle pushing out at the nose into the very tight ones. A gentle lifting of the throttle stops the pushing and, with the steering still so light in the hands and the car feeling so beautifully poised, it adheres to the line you wish it to follow, and you can then really push open the long-travel throttle and let the V8 propel you forward at a most pleasing rate. With such an introduction I was ready for the mountains ahead, and something close to 300 miles. Except for the few miles on the autostrada that took us between the two passes that we chose to negotiate and then back to Maranello when we had left the hills behind, except for them we were in series after series of bends; some hairpin-tight, others long and open. 'Most of the time I drove at a fast, steady pace so that Richard, my passenger, might not have to endure too much by way of g-force. Even so, it was quick enough pace for him to remark how exceptional, how extraordinary it seemed to be able to cover so many miles so quickly and easily and so obviously securely. For this little Dino is like that; one feels so relaxed in it. There seems to be plenty of time to position it correctly, to brake it, to steer it, to sweep it through the bends. One remains quite unflustered, even when you decide to use even more of the performance; to take it to 7700 rpm out of the bends, to come in hard and bloody fast under brakes, to approach the limits of the road-holding, to see if the balance can be upset. It can't. The Dino merely goes faster, swinging from one lock to the other with lightning response—and yet with gentleness—and outstanding precision. It's poise is never lost, its stability never upset. It feels so damned safe all the time. I would venture to suggest, with nothing more than what may be an unreliable memory as the measuring stick, that it has decidedly more roadholding than the 308GT4. And good as that car is, this is one notably better because it has such magnificent balance, and when it is going to go it gives you the warning, loud and clear, that the 2+2 doesn't; and it is easy to catch. This one is a jewel, an absolute honey; a fun car par excellence.'

Autocar's testers were a little less full blooded in their description:'While the handling has been praised generally, it would not be right to leave the subject without reference to throttle

Above *Protection against the elements. The padded fibreglass top of the 308GTS in position. When not in use it is stowed away behind the seats and can be encased in a vinyl waterproofed cover*

Left *With the top removed the car no longer appears to be so low*

61

Above and right US version 308GTS. Three-quarter front and rear views show why this car is such a good seller in a market where looks count almost as much as performance

open/throttle closed response. While the natural tendency is to understeer, if the accelerator is released in the mid-corner the resultant weight transfer does lead to an immediate tightening of the line. This is, of course, no penalty under most conditions (and can be used to advantage) but some caution is needed on wet or slippery roads. Once the natural understeer has been killed by lifting off the accelerator, immediate application of power can be used to set up a very satisfying four wheel drift which will please the skilled and

determined driver immensely. However, the relatively short wheelbase and low polar moment of inertia of the design mean that extreme angles of drift cannot be held despite the quickness and accuracy of the steering.'

Few general criticisms were made and most of those at points recognized as being minor ones. Some were old favourites. The heaviness of the clutch and the need to use its full travel was one. Nothing much had been done to reduce the number of turns of the steering wheel lock to

Above *Pre-taxying check. US version 308GTS with all flaps extended*

Top right *308GTS, US version. Engine shot shows the twin distributor electrics retained for USA; one of the air pumps forming part of the exhaust clean up system and the Vehicle Emission Control Information plate*

63

lock—3.3 turns—or the turning circle—still in the region of 40 ft. Paul Frère noted about the clutch that, at times, when it was hot after a series of standing start runs, the mechanism held the clutch pedal right down. This point had been made by an American writer about the GT4. Strongly criticised in one report was the choice of covering for the fascia. The reflections it produced in some lighting conditions were thought to be a hazard. When it rained the single cover over the engine/boot collected water which was promptly dumped over the engine and ignition when the cover was raised. Although the ignition didn't

Wide angle picture centres on 308GTS at final assembly

seem to object to such treatment a modification was later raised to give the plugs better protection.

Autocar published a full road test in their 23 October 1976 issue which provided the following figures.The weight of the car as tested was given as 3220 lb, a saving of 70 lb over that of the GT4. In terms of kerb weight the difference was even less, only 53 lb in favour of the fibreglass bodied GTB. Figures in brackets are from a *Car & Driver* June 1978 report on a 308GTS which for the American market, was rated lower (205 bhp at 6600 rpm) compared with the GTB's European 255 bhp at 7700 rpm. The kerb weight was 3290 lb.

mph	sec	mph	sec
0–30	2.3 (2.5)	0–80	10.8 (12.2)
0–40	3.3 (3.7)	0–90	13.8 (15.8)
0–50	5.1 (5.5)	0–100	17.0 (20.6)
0–60	6.5 (7.2)	0–110	20.4
0–70	8.8 (9.6)	0–120	25.0

In the top four gears:

mph	Top	4th	3rd	2nd	mph	Top	4th	3rd
10–30			5.1	3.3	70–90	7.7	5.5	4.4
20–40		6.4	4.1	2.7	80–100	8.8	6.0	
30–50	9.5	5.5	3.5	2.6	90–110	9.2	6.7	
40–60	8.4	5.0	3.6	4.8	100–120	10.2	8.0	
50–70	7.8	5.1	3.6					
60–80	7.2	5.1	3.9					

Standing quarter mile, 14.8 sec/93 mph (15.8 sec/90 mph): standing kilometre, 26.9 sec/124 mph. Maximum speeds in gears, 1st/44 mph, 2nd/65 mph, 3rd/92 mph, 4th/124 mph, 5th/154 mph. Fuel consumption figures by *Autocar* were very close to those for the GT4. Department of Transport gave, urban cycle-13.9 GTB/11.0 GTS; constant 56 mph—28.2 mpg, both and constant 75 mph—23.5, both.

CHAPTER 4

Fuel injection clears the air

Most of the changes made to the cars during their production life affected details rarely noted on their general specification.

Ferrari, along with all other automobile constructors, are faced with the problem of making and selling specialist cars in a world increasingly beset with legislation at all levels. These rules lay down standards of construction or performance sometimes in almost manic detail—which have to be met before a car is released to the general public. By no means the least of these are those affecting exhaust gas emissions. Lack of conformity with some of these had, insofar as the 12 cylinder engined cars were concerned, kept Ferrari from a number of potentially important markets.

To make a start at overcoming that situation, Bosch K Jetronic fuel injection was introduced on the V12 Type 400 during 1979. Not long after, similarly equipped versions of the 308GTB and 308GTS went into the catalogue. They became available in the US from around the middle of 1980; a few months later, the 308GTBi and 308GTSi as they are designated, were on sale in the United Kingdom. Along with the introduction of fuel injection, a number of other significant changes were made. These include the use of Marelli Digiplex electronic ignition; improved clutch operation; a modified gearbox with its own oil pump; changes to the interior trim, instruments and controls, and the fitting of Michelin TRX tyres. At the same time, wet-sump lubrication was standardized across the range.

Outwardly, little distinguished the revised models from those that had gone before. On both, the identifying script at the back now included an 'i' to denote the use of fuel injection. A closer look below the rear bumper revealed a new exhaust system with twin pipes either side of the silencer box. This last was not an infallible guide, as four pipe systems had been available as 'high performance' accessories for some time.

Amongst the various benefits claimed for fuel injection were improved cold starting, greater flexibility, elimination of fuel starvation under hard cornering, more uniform combustion, cleaner exhaust and no induction roar.

Bosch K Jetronic fuel injection, available for many years, has, because of its adaptability and simplicity of operation, been installed in many cars. It is a continuous injection system with

There is nothing from this angle to distinguish these US versions of the fuel injected 308GTSi and GTBi from the carburated models

*American specification
'injection' 308GTB compared
with European 308GTS. Note
bumpers and side marker
lights*

atomized fuel being sprayed into the inlet tract adjacent to the intake valves. It has the added advantage of not being engine driven. In spite of what its name may suggest, it is not an electronic system. The use of electricity is confined to operating a valve which enriches the mixture for cold starting and for heating a bi-metallic strip to weaken the mixture as the engine warms up.

In normal operation, fuel is delivered by an electrically driven roller cell type pump to a fuel accumulator before being filtered and passed onto the mixture control unit (MCU) which is the heart of the system. After leaving the MCU, fuel flows to the injector nozzles—one per cylinder. The principal components of the MCU are an air flow

308GTSi. Cockpit and controls. The clock and oil temperature gauge now form part of the central console. The switches for the electric windows have also been repositioned on to the console

sensor located ahead of the accelerator controlled throttle plate, a control plunger which operates to expose fuel metering slits and a system of diaphragm type delivery valves, one per cylinder, passing fuel to the injectors.

The air flow sensor takes the form of a plate which is attached to a balanced pivoting arm. It is free to move, according to the air flow conditions, within a cone shaped orifice the dimensions of which have been determined by the needs of the engine. The freedom of the sensor plate to adjust to variations in air flow through the orifice is governed by fuel pressure acting on the control plunger in contact with the balance arm of the sensor.

At each point in throttle opening a state of equilibrium is sought as the sensor plate moves to accommodate the change in air flow. In doing so it adjusts the position of the control plunger to vary the amount of fuel that can flow through the metering slits as these become either more or less exposed. The metered fuel passes to the delivery valves. These iron out any variations in pressure that may exist to ensure that the correct amount of fuel is delivered to the injector nozzles.

To aid cold starting the fuel accumulator delays the build up to full working pressure in the fuel system to temporarily reduce the pressure on the control plunger in the MCU. When the engine is switched off during or after a run, the accumulator maintains the working pressure for a limited period to assist hot starting.

The Marelli Digiplex system of electronic ignition incorporates a coil, a distributor head and an electronic module for each cylinder bank. The latter determine and apply the ignition advance needed to meet variations in engine load and speed. Engine load is deduced from the vacuum in the intake manifold. The measure of

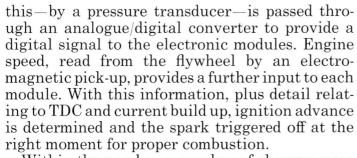

Above *Pop-up headlight detail*

Above left *Traffic jam view of the 308GTSi European version. Exhaust pipe outlets have reverted to twin type layout*

this—by a pressure transducer—is passed through an analogue/digital converter to provide a digital signal to the electronic modules. Engine speed, read from the flywheel by an electromagnetic pick-up, provides a further input to each module. With this information, plus detail relating to TDC and current build up, ignition advance is determined and the spark triggered off at the right moment for proper combustion.

Within the gearbox a number of changes were made, aimed at reducing the effort needed to change gear, lowering the level of noise in the box and improving the operation and reliability of the synchromesh. A system of forced lubrication was introduced by means of a pump driven from the output shaft. There were no significant changes to the individual ratios but the final drive was lowered from 3.706 to 4.06 This, taken in conjunction with a decrease in the laden radius of the Michelin TRX tyres, meant that the engine was revving higher for each road speed than before. The effort required to operate the clutch—subject of much criticism in the past—went down from 27 kg to 17 kg.

Michelin 220/55 VR 390 TRX on 165 mm rim Speedline wheels were standard. These put more rubber on the road from their increased width of 225 mm—19 mm more than that from the previous 205/70 VR 14 XWXs.

Somehow the interior trim of the 308GTB/GTS models had never seemed quite up to the level expected. On the 'i' versions a very definite improvement was visible.

The best Connolly leather was employed for the seats, the interior door trim, and the central console. The attention to detail and finish was excellent, with the consequence that much of the air of superb luxury exuded by the 400 series of V12s had been extended to the 308s. The doors had full leather trim, whereas on the previous models the loud speaker apertures were metal-faced. Along the lower part of the doors, a material similar to that used for the floor covering was used to protect the leather against scuffing.

An open weave material was used in some areas behind the seats and for the interior roof lining. In the roof of the GTB a lighting console was added to provide a general interior light and a more concentrated beam in its own swivel mounting, that could be used for map reading at night.

The instrumentation provided was the same as before but the face of the binnacle had a flat black finish rather than a brightly polished one. The clock and oil temperature gauges were removed from below the fascia and placed side by side on the console ahead of the gear change gate. The electric window switches are back on the console as well. The heater controls stayed but were revised to allow driver and passenger to select their own levels of heating. The slightly smaller diameter Nardi steering wheel had black spokes with black leather trim.

On the driver's side only, a more sensible

Left *Who says you can't go shopping in a Ferrari? Downtown America scene shows that you might need a little wider parking bay for ease of exit and entry*

Below *Window shopping— that well-known way of enjoying what at times we can't have*

rectangular shaped door mirror had been provided with an electrical adjustment from inside the car. A further sensible measure was the provision of a central door locking system.

The GTSi and GTBi are both credited with 214 bhp at 6600 rpm and 179 lb ft at 4600 rpm in European form. USA market figures were 205 bhp at 6600 rpm and 181 lb ft at 5000. It is doubtful whether in practice there was quite the fall off in power in Europe that these figures suggested, as requirements concerning stated power and so forth were becoming much more stringent than they had been.

By way of appraisal, *Car* magazine for June 1981 carried their findings from a back-to-back test of the GTBi-v-Lotus Turbo Esprit, and *Road & Track* have reported on their experiences with the GTSi version.

Against the Turbo Esprit, the Ferrari lost out on a number of small, detail points. In road holding and handling, *Car* felt that the Michelin TRX tyres took chassis-capability a considerable step forward, 'What the Michelins seem to do is to dramatically cut the old car's low speed tyre noise and to further 'tune' the chassis breakaway characteristics so that they are utterly predictable and quite graceful . . . . The throttle pedal controls it all. It is a little lighter than the one which in previous models controls a bank of Webers, but just as sensitive, progressive and entirely lacking in most motion. Approaching a 60 mph corner, near maximum effort. Let's say it understeers a whisker and you need to counter. In the Ferrari you have the option of merely pulling the nose in a whisker and continuing round with the front wheels still understeering a shade, or you can throttle off to a stage where the car moves beautifully into the shallowest of oversteer 'drifts' at which stage if you come back down on the power, you can keep the tail a shade out of line or exaggerate the angle with power—to the extent that it turns into a shallow power slide— according to your will.'

Road & Track after putting their car through slalom and skid pan tests, concluded that what they had previously regarded as a neutral handling car, now tended toward oversteer. Power-off brought the rear end further out, power-on broke the rear wheels loose causing the same reaction. Their tester felt 'This is not a car for the novice to drive on a winding, slippery road because it does not reward indecision'.

There was general agreement that the fuel injection fulfilled its promise of quieter running, better cold starting, freedom from fuel starvation when cornering, greater flexibility and a cleaner exhaust.

From the American car came the following acceleration figures: 0–30/2.9 sec, 0–50/6.1 sec, 0–60/7.9 sec, 0–70/10.6 sec, 0–80/13.4 sec and 0–100/22.1 sec. From the only figures quoted for the British tested car, it was 1.3 sec quicker up to 60 mph and 3.6 sec quicker out to 100 mph.

While the benefits of fuel injection were generally appreciated, there was disappointment that the cost of meeting legislative requirements was a publicly-stated curtailment of maximum power, along with loss of performance. It was a penalty that no manufacturer of high-performance cars could accept for long. Some means of restoring performance was needed to meet both the current situation and the longer-term future where legislation might become even more difficult to meet.

Turbocharging was an obvious solution, and Ferrari were no strangers to its demands and techniques. It had been forced upon them by the circumstances of Formula 1 racing in 1980 and (see chapter 5) had been adopted by the factory to offset the loss of power that had occurred with the introduction of a range of 2-litre V8s designed to take advantage of Italian tax law. But, to accept turbocharging to boost the power of the 308 series of cars would mean that apart from the V12-engined 400 series, all other models in the Ferrari catalogue would be turbocharged. However, that virtually 'all eggs in one basket' situation seemingly did not appeal to Ferrari any more than to other manufacturers. There was the possibility that more than a few potential customers might be put off by the adoption of bolt-on engineering where a modest increase in power would be sufficient to restore performance.

In those circumstances Ferrari could afford to look at a solution more fundamental to engine design and suitable for use with the conventional method of increasing power—a larger displacement engine—when that time might arrive. The press releases for the 1982 autumn round of motor shows were full of references to *quattrovalvole* by way of introducing the four-valves-per-cylinder Type F105 engine that would be used for future 308 cars. Maximum power was brought up to 240 bhp

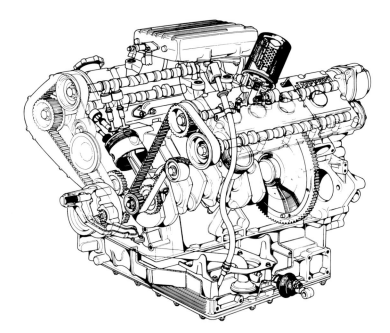

Right *The theory is that four lightweight valves can be operated at higher engine speeds to produce more power*

Below *The naked four-valve cylinder head as fitted to the Type F105 engine and made from an aluminium-silicon alloy*

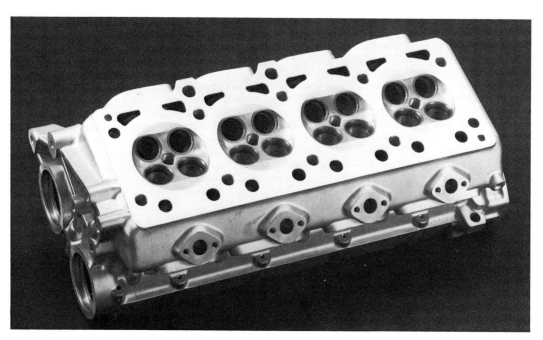

at the slightly increased figure of 7000 rpm and peak torque increased to 191 lb ft at 5000 rpm.

Traditional multi-valve theory allows that smaller valves can—by virtue of their lighter weight—be operated at higher engine speeds to produce more power. Ferrari chose to ignore that potential by retaining for the newer engine the 7700 rpm limit laid down for the earlier versions. The smaller valve lift associated with the decrease in valve head diameter, and the reduction in the included angle between opposing valves from 46 degrees to 33 degrees, undoubtedly improved porting and allowed the CR to be raised from 8.8 to 9.2:1. Writing in his review of the new engine 'Four Over Eight' in the February 1983 issue of *Car*, Leonard Setright suggested that a feature of valve performance theory known as 'curtain area', which was 38 per cent greater on the inlet side of the four valve heads than on the

With a rise in compression ratio from 8.8 to 9.2:1, maximum power rose from 230 to 240 bhp

Right *The major body changes were made at the front where a new grille with daylight flashers appeared, as did a bonnet ventilation panel*

Below *At the rear, the model designation was changed for both GTB and GTS to 308 quattrovalvole*

original two-valve layout, was largely responsible for a significantly greater charge intake with a beneficial effect upon performance.

The opportunity was taken to introduce some additional detail changes into the engine. The most notable of these was the adoption of aluminium nikasil-faced liners in place of the original cast-iron ones. The pistons were also redesigned with flat dished heads.

Very little was done to the body of the car that would instantly identify it as a new model. At the front the radiator grille was modified. Daylight flasher units were installed on either side, immediately below the indicator/parking lights which remained set into the bumper. An almost full-width ventilation panel was set well forward in the bonnet cover. At the rear the model desig-

A new option was the roof-mounted spoiler just visible in this front-three-quarters studio shot

nation script for both the GTB and GTS versions was changed to '308 quattrovalvole'. An optional roof-mounted (behind the cockpit) spoiler was available for both models.

The all-important question of whether performance had been restored was answered, insofar as European-specification cars were concerned, by the road test report on a 308GTB Qv which appeared in the 29 October 1983 issue of *Motor*. However, *Car & Driver* provided an answer on behalf of the American-version cars in their August 1983 issue which was not so flattering as the *Motor* report. There appeared, from the data panel, to be differences in specification that helped the imbalance. The USA car was rated 230 bhp at 6800 rpm and 188 lb ft of torque at 5500 rpm. The engine compression ratio was lower at 8.6:1, and there was a 4.06 final drive ratio instead of the 3.823 of the European car. In the following table, the USA report figures, where applicable, are shown in brackets.

mph	sec	mph	sec
0–30	2.1 (2.3)	0–80	9.2 (11.5)
0–40	3.0 (3.5)	0–90	11.6 (15.1)
0–50	4.5 (5.3)	0–100	14.3 (18.5)
0–60	5.7 (7.4)	0–110	17.2 (23.3)
0–70	7.5 (9.2)	0–120	20.5 (32.0)

In the top two gears:

mph	Top	4th
20–40	8.1	5.5
30–40	7.4	5.0
40–60	7.3	5.1
50–70	7.2	5.1
60–80	7.3	5.1
70–90	7.4	5.1
80–100	7.4	5.1
90–110	8.0	5.7

*Bertone's body together with
Ferrari's first use of a V8
engine in a production car
did nothing to satisfy the
traditionalist. In fact, the
308GT4 is an excellent 2+2
now gaining favour*

Above *This American
specification 308GT4
bodyshell awaits more
mechanicals at the Ferrari
factory in 1977*

Top *Pininfarina's 308GTB
was launched to rave
reviews, at least about its
looks. This time everyone was
right—it's an outstanding
beauty (US spec.)*

Right *Peter Coltrin
photography at its best.
Although all Ferraris are
developed extensively on the
track, the 308GTB has
virtually no racing record*

Right *308GTS at Donington during a test session. Note deeper front spoiler and later four pipe exhaust previously reserved for American customers*

Below *Metres of Connolly hide trim the interiors of most 308s. This is an early 308GTSi. Steering wheel is signed by Mr Nardi*

Left *Pre-launch shot of the Mondial 8 at Fiorano, Ferrari's own test track, actually one of the most sophisticated in the business. The shape of the new car should grow on you*

Below left *America is without question Ferrari's most important market. Extended noses and side marker lights confirm the territory of this pair: 308GTBi and Mondial 8*

Below *Mondial 8. There's no direct connection with its famous forebear, hence the addition of the '8'*

*This cutaway illustration of
the 3.2 Mondial shows that
despite the mid-engined
configuration there is
reasonable space for both
passengers and their luggage*

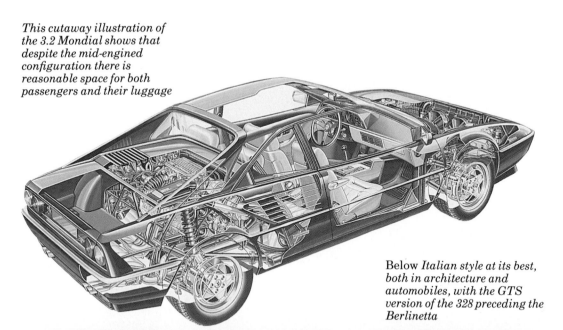

Below *Italian style at its best,
both in architecture and
automobiles, with the GTS
version of the 328 preceding the
Berlinetta*

CHAPTER 5

Turbocharging

Although Ferrari elected not to introduce turbocharging as a means of increasing the power of the 308-series cars, they had not ruled it out of favour for certain applications of their V8 range of engines. The most powerful of these had been the engine developed for use by Lancia in their Group C cars, intended to compete in the World Endurance Championship series of races in 1983. The 2955 cc engines with their twin KKK turbochargers were putting out around 620 bhp at race boost pressures. At the 54th Geneva Salon in 1984, Ferrari unveiled their new 'GTO'. The 2.8-litre V8 engine employed twin Japanese IHI turbos to achieve its road-going power of 400 bhp. The car was scheduled for limited production—enough to achieve homologation as a Group B car—at which point a number of so-called evolutionary cars were to be built for competition use.

Both of these applications lie well outside the scope of this book. Much closer has been the use of turbocharging to boost the power of the 208 series of cars. As far back as 1975, Ferrari had introduced a 2-litre version of the GT4 in order to boost sales at home, where the sales tax on cars doubles (from 18 to 36 per cent of the list price) when the engine displacement exceeds 2 litres. In due course, the 208GT4 gave way to 2-litre versions of the GTB/GTS range. The problem with

Above *The home-market 208 Turbo with NACA duct and roof spoiler*

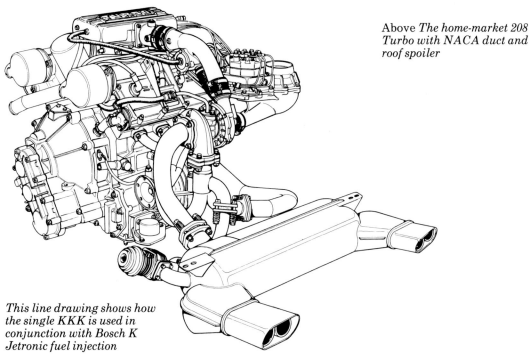

This line drawing shows how the single KKK is used in conjunction with Bosch K Jetronic fuel injection

all of these smaller-engined cars was that the power produced—170 bhp for the GT4, falling to 155 bhp for the GTB/GTS—had to propel vehicles that were identical in size, shape and weight to the 3-litre-engined versions. Performance naturally suffered and sales dropped. With a substantial increase in power required for a limited and local application, Ferrari were seemingly happy to go for turbocharging to do the job. At the 1982 Turin Auto Show, the 208 Turbo was introduced. A single KKK (Kuhnle, Kopp and Kausche) unit, the K26 model, was used in conjunction with the Bosch K Jetronic fuel injection. The compression ratio of the engine was lowered to 7:1. The turbo boost was set at 0.6 bar/8.8 psi. Maximum power was given as 220 bhp at 7000 rpm, which brought the smaller-engined cars up to around the same level as the fuel-injected 308s. Recently, with the introduction of the 328 range, there have been modifications to the 208s to

Turin Show 1982. Ferrari unveils the 208 Turbo. The giveaway in this shot is the NACA duct low down on the body ahead of the rear wheel arch

enable them to stay in touch. The KKK turbocharger has been replaced by a Japanese IHI unit which has a maximum boost of 1.05 bar/15.4 psi. This has been combined with a heat exchanger unit, located between the compressor outlet and the intake manifold, to cool the ingoing charge, and other detail changes to produce an output of 254 bhp at 6500 rpm.

While the 208 Turbo was under development as a catalogue model, Ferrari's UK importer, Maranello Concessionaires, turbocharged a 308GTB as a practical way of finding out what it was all about.

The car chosen was a—year old at the time—carburetted-version GTB. The work was carried out by Janspeed Engineering who spent several months developing it in order to match reliability with speed and, as far as possible, to ensure that the process could be repeated without headaches on customer cars.

Before settling for a single turbocharger, Janspeed investigated the possibility of using a

208 Turbo. For lovers of pipework the engine of the turbo Ferrari will give hours of pleasure. Have you figured out how it all works yet?

Left *Even the luggage is marked 'Turbo'*

Below *Underbonnet view of Janspeed's blow-through single-turbo conversion for the 308*

Above *The silencer was hidden away under the rear tray and the tailpipe exited in the usual place. In all, a neat installation*

Right *Janspeed located the wastegate between the exhaust pipe and the drive housing*

twin layout, in line with what the factory were said to have under consideration. Apparently there was room in the engine compartment for this to be done, but it was ruled out on grounds of cost and—at the time—the lack of a smaller capacity turbocharger.

The 308 Turbo used a Garrett T04 turbocharger mounted high behind the engine on a specially made exhaust manifold which took exhaust from the front cylinder bank exhaust. Air, drawn in through a filtered box at the right rear of the engine compartment, was put through the turbo-charger and then via an induction pipe, to a flat rectangular chamber above the four twin-choke Weber carburettors which remained on the standard inlet manifold. The 8.8:1 compression ratio was that of the standard car. Its retention meant that off-the-boost performance was not lacking. Pre-ignition problems, which might have occurred through a combination of that compression ratio and turbo heated air, were taken care of by inter-cooling. This was accomplished by circulating freon from the car's air conditioning system through a radiator matrix, which formed part of the air box over the carburettors. Circulation of the freon started when a pressure switch, sensing the onset of turbo boost, operated a magnetic clutch on the air conditioning pump.

The carburettors were special, sealed-spindle versions of the 40DCNF Webers normally used. Apparently, with blow-through turbocharging, the fuel-air mixture removes lubrication from the butterfly spindles which then wear rapidly. The turbocharger unit had its own lubrication system consisting of a pump driven from the inlet cam-shaft of the rear bank, a sump, a cooling radiator, pressure light, and oil temperature gauge. The amount of boost was limited to 5.25 psi by a waste-gate on the induction pipe. Higher boost was

Top right Janspeed carried out another attempt at turbocharging, this time with twin turbos. It was even neater with chromed pipework and castings to match those of Ferrari. The conversion was carried out on David Powell's Mondial Qv

Bottom right The amount of hardware needed for the twin-turbo installation is quite extensive and it includes the inter-cooler seen on the left

tried, but brought on pre-ignition problems for a very limited increase in performance.

No power figures were released for the turbocharged engine, but an extra 40 bhp was claimed. If we accept that the actual power from a carburetted 308 was probably nearer 230 bhp than the claimed 255, this put the turbo some 60 bhp up on a regular fuel-injected GTB.

Car magazine spent a few days with the car and in their report of October 1981 said: 'What, then, about the performance? The engine starts in a similar manner to the fuel-injected 308—no choke, no pumping of the accelerator. On test, we often found the car hard to start from cold; it would fire instantly, but it wouldn't catch. If you use choke you flood the carburettors. Even when warm, the engine won't burst into life with the exultancy of an all-Ferrari 308. But once it's running evenly, it is very, very smooth and there are none of the hiccups of the usual cold engine. It's silken.

'And it's powerful. There is such push from the engine—realistically speaking, probably 60–70 bhp, stronger than that of a 308/GTBi, that the driver is hard-worked just to manipulate the clutch and gearchange fast enough. The injected car has a longer, more easily wielded gear lever and a lighter clutch. A 308 Turbo driver could often do with both.

'The 308 Turbo, even with its Michelin XWX tyres on optional 7.5 in. wide wheels (the standard wheels are 6.5 in.) will spin its wheels with determination if the clutch is popped in the turbocharger's operating band. Then it arrows down the road, front wheels light and nose high, in comparative silence but propelled by power enough to match a Turbo Esprit. In the longer gears, at full throttle, the boost gauge starts to register positively at about 2900 rpm. It provides

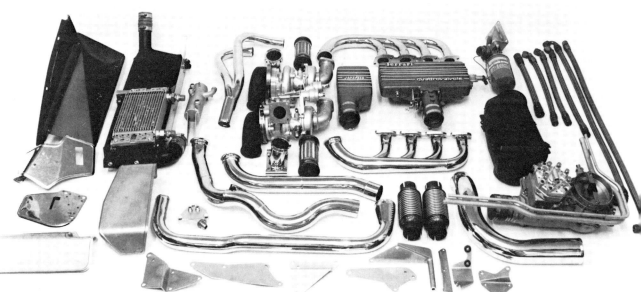

its maximum blow of 5.25 psi at about 4400 rpm. From there up—a further band of 3300 rpm—the power is massive, smooth, effortless, long-legged and quiet in a way no 308 has been before.

'We never reached this Turbo's maximum speed. We merely discovered that at a genuine 150 there was more to come, so much more that we felt that the engine might even spin to its 7700 rpm redline and 165 mph! But all this performance comes at the expense of high fuel consumption. We ran several checks, some when using the potential and others when treading carefully. Our best figure, over 170 miles on open roads, was 14.1 mpg. This fell to only 11.8 when the turbocharger was regularly doing its work. That's no better than a Boxer returns and certainly somewhat worse than either an injected or carburettor 308 would return.'

They went on to ask: 'It might seem—it seemed to us at first—that to give a proven 150 mph car a lot more potential is a patent waste of fuel and enterprise. Yet the extra power can be used in a surprising number of places. You use it uphill for consuming lines of crawling cars (where you can't have too much power). You use it to boot the car out of bends on the limit of its rear adhesion (not nearly so easily reached with the standard power). And the extra potential suits the more relaxed, high gearing of the carburettor 308s; it was lowered from 21.7 mph/1000 rpm in top to 19.3 mph for the 308/GTBi to compensate for the GTBi's lower, 210 bhp power output.

'So great is the extra cornering kick out of bends that Maranello Concessionaires have found it advisable to fit stiffer shock absorbers to this pilot car. It does stay rigidly, ruthlessly flat, now, even in S-bends which might otherwise set up a modest body lurch. The ride is still good; flat and completely lacking in untoward bounce, but there is more bump-thump than we remember of recent 308s, part of it doubtlessly due to this firmer damping and part to the inferior bump absorption properties of the older XWX tyres.'

The question of reliability remained unanswered. Janspeed guaranteed the reliability of the components they fitted and the quality of their workmanship. There would obviously have been a very big 'X' factor, however, if the conversion had been carried out to other than a completely new or 'fully-known-history' car.

The low effort in the UK contrasted with the situation in the USA, where turbocharging conversions were regularly advertised and available.

The 308 owner in the US had the choice of two major suppliers of kits. Each, according to reports, had its 'best application'. The Ameritech kit was reckoned to be eminently suited to the carburetted cars and the BAE to the fuel-injected versions. Installation time for the 114-part Ameritech kit was said to be 35 hours, and the hardware that was provided left very little of the original intake and exhaust systems.

On the inlet side the four Weber carburettors were removed from the engine vee and replaced by a four-legged cast-aluminium manifold. A tapered snout extending rearward and downward from the manifold joined up with a Rajay 375E turbocharger mounted adjacent to the rearmost cylinder head. The fuel-air mixture was delivered by a modified Carter AFB 9400 four-barrel carburettor which had been laboratory jetted to eliminate the need for adjustment at installation.

On the exhaust side the only original parts remaining were the manifolds, and they had been insulated to minimize heat loss. A stainless steel silencer, without trace of a catalytic converter and discharging through single outlets, one either side, replaced the original system. The maximum boost was limited by a wastegate set to operate at 6 psi, although some reports put the figure at 8 psi. To avoid detonation, the carburettor was set for a rich mixture under high loads and the ignition advance curve changed to limit the total advance to 35 degrees compared to the 36 degrees that is normal. For the 30 or so hours of work put in at installation, it was estimated that an additional 115 bhp and 120 lb ft of torque were available.

There was the usual spread of test data. *Car & Driver* in their August 1981 write-up gave a 0–60 mph figure of 5.7 sec; 0–100 mph in 13.8 sec and a standing quarter mile of 14.3 sec for 102 mph. An *Autoweek* report gave a 0–60 time of 4.8 sec—consistently achieved—and a standing quarter mile of 13.5 sec for 108 mph.

The BAE kit was aimed specifically at the fuel-injected 308s and, by bringing in the turbocharger's compressor between the fuel-injection

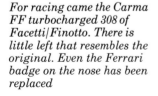

For racing came the Carma FF turbocharged 308 of Facetti/Finotto. There is little left that resembles the original. Even the Ferrari badge on the nose has been replaced

metering unit and the standard intake manifold, was said to have saved most of the original factory items on the intake side. A complete exhaust system, including a catalytic converter, was provided as part of the kit. Presumably because of the amount of original items still usable, the time of installation was about a quarter of that for the Ameritech kit.

Power was said to be up to 287 bhp against a quoted, but rather low, figure of 180 bhp for the stock 308GTBi. The turbo's 0–60 acceleration time was given as 6.0 sec (7.9 stock) and a standing quarter mile of 14.3 sec for 95 mph (15.9 sec for 87.7 mph stock).

Carma FF 308 in practice. Such sessions were often its finest moments

Mondial 8— a significant addition

The 308 story, which started with a 2+2 GT4 in 1973, came, through the introduction of the Mondial 8 at the Geneva Show of 1980, full circle. In naming the car, Ferrari departed from their normal method of type designation by the capacity of a single cylinder. They also reached back into their sporting past for the name 'Mondial', which had previously been used for a four-cylinder sports racer built in 1954.

In an early brochure on the Mondial, Ferrari were specific about its purpose: 'The Mondial 8 is aimed at widening the scope of Ferrari's market by offering a package combining the features of a genuine sports car with a comfortable GT. In the last few years, the market for high performance cars has undergone major changes with those new models featuring enhanced versatility and reliability proving most successful. Today's motorists expect in a sports car the comfort and appointments of a de luxe saloon, in addition to performance and style. The Mondial 8 while fully meeting these requirements is aimed at a much wider market. The results of a recent investigation have shown that buyers of a Ferrari model are extremely diversified and that they drive their cars daily with an annual mileage of even 30 thousand kilometres.'

Also made clear was the importance attached

to the American market where, it was stated, 35 per cent of production went. To that end, the Mondial had been engineered to meet federal requirements for active and passive safety as well as for environmental protection.

In an interview for *Symbol* magazine, Leonardo Fioravanti, director of the Pininfarina Research Unit, discussed his objectives thus: 'It was a very difficult project. We had to design 2 + 2 bodywork for a vehicle with a central engine; in other words, we had to accommodate real space for four people according to specific mechanical conditions that made the overall space solution a somewhat delicate matter. This had to be without, obviously, forgetting that the vehicle had to have the long, sleek styling typical of all Ferrari cars.'

Essentially the Mondial's mechanics were the same as those of the fuel-injected 308s, apart from some detail changes, and one important chassis difference which broke new ground for Ferrari. For the Mondial a separate chassis subframe at the rear carried the engine, transmission and suspension. This subframe assembly could be unbolted and removed from the car as an aid to easier servicing. The fuel tanks were removed from the engine compartment and placed underneath the rear seats. Modifications were made to the front suspension to reduce steering kickback and introduce a degree of anti-dive under braking. The tyres were Michelin TRX 240/55 VR 390 on 180 TR × 390 rims. In the construction of the car, more use was made of ribbed and boxed steel stampings, and very much more attention paid to corrosion prevention.

Pininfarina styling, subject to the usual reservations that accompany 2 + 2s, was well received. Most recognized that this type of body offered the stylist little room for manoeuvre if serious consideration was to be given to accom-

103

Early classic. 1953 Mondial 500. The body on this four cylinder competition sports car was both designed and built by Pininfarina

modating four people in comfort. In profile the Mondial was both striking and well proportioned. Most of the criticisms made were directed against the large air intakes on the sides. Originally accentuated by being picked out in black, they were eventually made to match the surrounding paintwork, thereby becoming a little less noticeable.

At the rear of the car there was a return to separate covers for engine compartment and boot. The rear light clusters were the same as for the

308GTB/GTS, but let into a skirt below the rear
bumper were a pair of rectangular-shaped red fog
lights. At the front, flashers for daylight use were
worked into the bumper, while the pop-up main
lamp units reverted to the twin light arrangement
of the 308GT4.

A real attempt was made by the Pininfarina
designers to seat four people comfortably. As a
result, the Mondial was much roomier inside than
its GT4 predecessor, the outcome of a skilful
exploitation of some modest additions—100 mm

wheelbase, 280 mm overall length, 80 mm overall width and 30 mm overall height—to the GT4's dimensions.

Before lengthening the wheelbase, the assurance of Ferrari engineers that this would not adversely affect the car's handling was sought.

Opinion naturally varied as to whether the car was a true 2+2. Undoubtedly there was now sufficient room for two adults—'above average size', reports say—to sit in tandem on the passenger side of the car. On the other side, the comfort of the fourth person very much depended on the positioning of the driver's seat. To help the driver, the steering wheel was adjustable for both reach and tilt.

All necessary instruments were grouped together in a rectangular-shaped binnacle

Prototype Mondial 8 on test

directly ahead of the driver. In right-hand-drive cars, the rev counter was to the left with the speedometer on the right. Between them was a vertical, double banked display of the usual warning lights. To the right of the speedometer, a group of six switches operated the front and rear fog lights, the engine, boot and front bonnet covers, and the heated rear window. To the left of the rev counter, four dials covered engine oil temperature and pressure, water temperature and fuel level. Between these and the rev counter there was a digital read-out clock. The controls for heating and ventilation were in a separate panel to the left of the driver and below the fascia. Five switches on the central console behind the gear lever gate raised and lowered the windows, switched on the parking lights, adjusted the outside mirror and opened the fuel filler cover.

Geneva Show 1980. Presentation of the Mondial 8. It came in the year that Pininfarina celebrated 50 years of design

In what some considered to be an excess of electronic gimmickry—although there were more complaints about execution than concept—electronic monitoring of certain vital information was introduced.

This operated through sensors to illuminate a series of warning panels. These covered low coolant level; failure of the brake-fluid-level warning light; unlocked bonnet or boot; low level of engine or transmission oil; low level screenwash; car overdue for next service; stop light

failure; failure of driving lamps; and lack of freon in the air conditioner. Each time the engine was switched on, a red panel would light up if a failure was recorded for one of the first four items; other failures were recorded by the illumination of a yellow panel. A green light showed if all was correct. The main complaints about the system were that it was awkwardly situated. Thus in some daylight conditions it was very difficult to be sure whether a fault was being indicated or not.

Acceptable as the car generally was from styl-

Publicity shot for the Mondial 8 shows amongst other features the reversion to twin light pop-up units

ing and finishing standpoints, it came in for considerable adverse comment—particularly from American testers—on its acceleration capabilities. But in many other respects it was obviously much better suited to its expected mode of use.

With the introduction of fuel injection, the power and torque realized from the 308 engine dropped for the GTBi/GTSi versions to 214 bhp/ 179 lb ft in Europe and 205 bhp/181 lb ft in America. With the Mondial using the same engine, the drop in power was up against, on the one hand, an increase in weight and, on the other, increased frontal area resulting from the additional width and height. The weight increase was in the region of 400 lb plus. The Americans were having to settle for a 0–60 mph figure of 8.20 sec best (9.3 average) and a 0–100 mph in the region of 28.0 sec. In the UK corresponding figures were probably between 7 and 8 and just over 21 seconds. In these legislated days, environmental protection, com-

Mondial 8. This three-quarter rear view shows the general appearance of the car quite well. Apart from the air intake grilles there has been little criticism of Pininfarina's design. Most people now recognize the limitations placed on the stylist by practical 2 + 2s

Above *Mondial 8 open for inspection*

Left *Difficult to judge from this photo, the interior is much improved from earlier cars in the 308 series. Rear seating is also much more comfortable*

Above *Note that on this US registered Mondial 8 the air intake grilles are the same colour as the body. There are also some differences below the bumper*

Left *Mondial 8 cockpit. Instrumentation is a little mundane*

fort and extremes of performance are not good bedfellows.

If there was disappointment with the traffic-light GP potential, there were compensations in more important areas. *Motor* in their report of 5 December 1981 noted: 'Where the Mondial really shines is in its chassis. Like the GTB and the GT4 before it, the steering is initially unendearing, managing to feel low-geared yet excessively heavy at parking speeds. Through tight, low speed corners taken gently, the Mondial seems to under-steer too, calling for a degree of wheel twirling that hardly augurs well for when you start trying. How misleading those initial impressions are! When you corner quickly, particularly on fast curves, when the car is developing some real weight transfer, the feeling of understeer all but disappears, the chassis becomes alive with feel—it almost seems as if the car can defy the laws of motion, so great is the lateral acceleration that can be developed. The revisions to the front sus-pension certainly have reduced steering kickback from the thumb-cracking level though there's still a little too much on really bumpy surfaces. But the kickback does help endow—and the TRX tyres too, no doubt—the Mondial with a feel of a quality (dare I say Porsche-like quality?) hitherto lacking in Ferraris. On a twisting country road, the steering writhes gently in your hands, letting there be no doubt of the state of the road under the front wheels.

'Enter a corner too quickly and lifting the throttle produces a mild tightening of the line—enough to scrub speed off without requiring a spe-cific steering correction—and even if you're forced to brake in mid-corner, hard, the Mondial slows without an excessive change of attitude. This stability is one of the Mondial's fortes and the Ferrari engineers deserve the greatest compli-

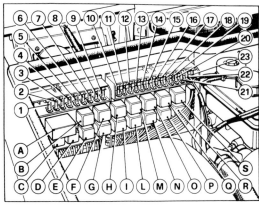

ment for managing to blend such good high speed stability (even at 120 mph on a bumpy country road with the wheels pounding up and down like pistons the Mondial feels rock-solid on line) with a lack of understeer and neutrality in strong cornering.

'The scale of the Maranello chassis team's achievement becomes even more evident when the excellent ride is taken into account, and the unusually good (for this class of car) suppression of road noise. The Mondial does feel firm and jiggly at low speed, though never uncomfortable as any vertical jarring has been cunningly removed by subtle tuning of the dampers. At speed, over all surfaces, the ride smooths out to become more than acceptable—on motorway and smooth A-roads it almost qualifies for the magic carpet class.

'The only time where caution is needed is on slippery surfaces such as damp leaves (it didn't rain during our test) where excessive throttle can make the tail step out of line very smartly indeed. You have to be very quick and accurate applying opposite lock, though just the right amount of castor action is a considerable help.

'Matching this superb road behaviour is a braking system that must be as good as that of any road car in the world today. Massive ventilated disc brakes larger at the rear (11.78 in.) than at the front (11.0 in.) in deference to the car's rearward weight bias and a vacuum servo provide a progressive and positive pedal action, whether the brakes are hot or cold.'

While it is always difficult to sum up a 2+2 Ferrari, *Motor Sport* were perhaps near the mark when they said, at the time: 'It's not the quickest car available for the money, but it's about as well finished as you could wish and offers the indefinable magic of Ferrari motoring as an every day

Above left *Mondial 8 bodyshell starting to pick up vital hardware*

Below left *A degree in electronics may help. Fuses and relays you may have to cope with one dark night*

Below right *Interior shot on Mondial 8 suggests much improved room in the back*

Above *Mondial quattrovalvole, possibly the first of the V8s to utilize the four-valve heads. Outwardly it was almost unchanged*

Right *Inside, however, there were extensive changes to the fascia and to the rear seats which were made to fold flat*

Below *Ferrari found instant success by cutting the roof off and calling it a Cabriolet*

experience rather than as an occasional treat.'

In spite of the adverse criticism aimed—a little unfairly in view of its purpose—at the Mondial 8, Ferrari kept the car in production, advanced its specification in line with the rest of the 308 series, and introduced a Cabriolet version—the first regular Cabriolet to be put into production by them since the early 1970s.

A four-valve version of the Mondial was introduced in August 1982, which was possibly the first of the V8s to carry the new engine. Outwardly, little distinguished the new version from its predecessor. At the rear the model designation script was changed to read 'Mondial quattrovalvole'. Within the cockpit the central console was modified by extending it forward and installing a radio in the extension. At the same time, the display panel monitoring various levels, and so on, was turned through 90 degrees and moved forward to lie alongside the gear lever where its information would better catch the driver's eye.

The Cabriolet version was introduced in October 1983. It has been said that the intention at the time was that it would be available only to the American market, but by putting one into the Brussels Show in 1984, Ferrari made it clear that European customers would also be catered for.

The new car won instant acclaim. Removal of the roof brought into greater prominence the gentle curves of the upper body which flowed from the bumper, up over the front wheels, flattened out in the region of the doors, before rising over the rear wheels and easing down to the tail. The large swept-back front windshield, also coming down into its own, added a forward thrust to the car.

By most accounts, the folding top was not too much of a problem to get up or to stow away after

Right *A squirt of sealer adds that all-important finishing touch to the Mondial Cabriolet*

Below *Power curves for the quattrovalvole engine*

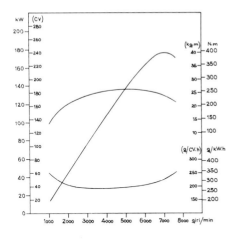

use. In a neat arrangement, Pininfarina left a part of each of the original sail panels in place and duplicated that shape with the protective boot. Another interesting feature was the retractable, electrically-operated, quarter windows behind the doors that could be raised when the top was up. To increase the amount of luggage space available, the backs of the rear seats were made to fold down on to the seat cushions.

The elegance of line, combined with the boost in performance available from the four-valve engine, brought forth the praise that had been muted when the Mondial 8 had been introduced some three to four years previously.

CHAPTER 7

Ferrari 328

If success or failure bring problems in their wake, those of the latter may at times be the easier to solve because 'back to the drawing-board' often allows a clean sweep to be made. Success, though, poses the question of how to hang on to it and exploit it to the best advantage.

When Ferrari introduced the V8 engine into their range of GT cars, they could hardly have foreseen that 12 years later the 308 would still be in use as a model designator, and that in that space of time they would have built just over 16,000 308s in a production exceeding the 12,600 cars produced in total from 1947 to 1973. Allowing for other models, 45 per cent of Ferrari total production since 1947 was attributable to the 308 series. Although there have been occasional shaky patches, Ferrari have always been able to sell all the cars they have made. So, with the continuing success of the 308s, there was little direct incentive to change direction beyond the fact that the market place thrives on change, though not necessarily dramatic change.

The rumours that normally abound when a new Ferrari is in the offing pointed to a retention of the V8 solution, but left open the question of whether technology would again intervene—there was still turbocharging—or whether there would be a reversion to the good old-fashioned method of increased capacity. Porsche had done just that with the introduction of a 3.2-litre version of their old favourite, the 911.

When late in 1985 the 328 series of cars was announced, it was seen that the 'old-fashioned' approach had won the day. In appearance the new cars are close to the 308 range, but with sufficient detail changes to distinguish old from new. The opportunity has also been taken to refine some of the engineering.

The increased capacity comes from a change in the bore and stroke dimensions to 83×73.6 mm for a true capacity of 3185 cc—an increase of 8.8 per cent. Maximum power has gone up by 12.5 per cent from 240 bhp to 270 bhp, with specific power up to 84.7 bhp/litre from its previous figure of 81.9. The engine speed for maximum power stays at 7000 rpm. The maximum torque figure, previously 191 lb ft, has gone up to 223 lb ft and at the higher speed of 5500 rpm. Valve timing remains the same as for the 'Qv' cars, but a revised camshaft on the inlet side gives greater lift. The pistons, which are new, have been designed to give a 'squish' effect as an aid to improving combustion, a process given further impetus by the use of smaller (12 mm) spark plugs with improved location.

A further refinement replaces the Marelli Digiplex system of ignition with that firm's more versatile Microplex system already specified for the flat-12 engined Testarossa.

To cope with the increased level of performance henceforth on tap, new oil radiators with greater cooling surface have been introduced. Within the transmission individual gear ratios remain, but there is a change in the overall ratios through the introduction of a 17/63 crown wheel and pinion in place of the 17/65 set used for the Qv cars.

In a carry-over from the Mondial Qv where, insofar as the 308/Mondial cars are concerned, it

Rather than turn to turbocharging, Ferrari chose to increase capacity in their efforts to extract more power from the V8

was introduced shortly after production of that model started, the handbrake now operates through conventional brake shoes which open out on to the interior of the brake discs. Standard wheels are now 7 × 16 in. rims with 205/55 VR16 tyres at the front, and 8 × 16 in. rims with 225/50 VR16 tyres at the rear.

The external appearance of the 328s is clearly a further refinement of the 308 cars. In profile they have lost much of the sharpness at the front that came from below the bumper line, where the steep rearward angle of the lower fairing was followed by the forward thrust of the spoiler. A new and stronger bumper, colour keyed to the body and formed as an integral part of the lower fairing,

has been devised; it is not as deep nor as noticeably forward as that of the 308's. Below it the fairing slopes gently towards the rear of the car. The separate spoiler, much less aggressive in appearance, is grilled to admit air into the forward part of the car. The front grille, now more prominent, is not as wide because the new light clusters which combine parking, direction indicating and daylight flashing—a hand-on from the Testarossa—take up room at either side. The vents behind the light pods in the front wheel arches have gone and those in the bonnet cover have been moved forward and deepened.

Like that at the front, the rear bumper is formed as part of the lower fairing and colour matched to the body of the car. It would appear to offer a useful first line of contact against those who, in hot pursuit of a Ferrari, may not be as well braked in an emergency. The rear fog lights are let into the lower fairing. Below, a grille across the back of the car now hides all of the exhaust system, with the exception of the twin pipes.

The cockpit has undergone a number of changes. Immediately noticeable are the new spade-grip-type door handles—separated from the arm rests, which on the driver's side incorporate switches for raising and lowering the windows on both sides, plus adjustment for the exterior mirrors. On the passenger side the switch adjusts only the window. The handbrake lever has been removed from the centre to a position between the driver's seat and door. That has allowed some redesign of the central console to incorporate a glove-box compartment where the handbrake lever used to be. The metal toggle-type switches have given way to the flat touch type. The herring-bone pattern panels of the seats in the 308 Qvs have been replaced by rectangular panelling on the 328s.

Top left *Externally the 328 is a refinement of the 308. Much of the sharpness at the front has been lost with the new grille treatment*

Centre left *At the front a new grille with Testarossa-style light cluster and the absence of vents behind the headlight pods*

Bottom left *At the rear the bumper, like that at the front, is now integral and colour coded, and a grille with reversing lights hides the exhaust system*

Top *Inside there are several detail changes to the console, handbrake lever and furniture*

Centre *The Mondial 3.2 models have also undergone extensive but subtle restyling, most noticeable being the addition of new convex wheels*

Right *The bodywork has received similar smoothing and rounding, particularly below the belt line, in line with the other models.*

The impressions gathered by Steve Cropley in his report on a 328GTB in the July issue of *Car*, and the more detailed figures given by *Motor* in their road test report on a similar model in the 21 June 1986 issue, made it very clear that here—in their opinion—is a Ferrari that will do a genuine 160 mph and with a mid-range performance that is outstanding. Cropley makes the point that, 'the Ferrari is now a genuine 160 mph car. It will pull that speed on any old stretch of unrestricted autobahn. In fact, it will pull its maximum engine speed, 7700 rpm in top, with surprising ease. . . .' *Motor* confirmed this with a top speed of 158.8 mph round the high-speed bowl of the Motor Industry Research Association (MIRA) facility at Millbrook and a fastest-leg speed of 161.2 mph.

Of the important mid-range performance, *Car* said: 'This engine has so much mid-range urge that you can easily miss second altogether and go just as quickly. . . . The 328 will sprint to 60 mph in just 5.8 sec, which used to be a good time for a Countach until the latest 475 bhp version came along. And even though third won't pull to 100 mph—and three gear changes are therefore included in the time—the car will just beat 14 sec to 100 mph, which is Boxer territory too. Even when you select top to venture beyond 120 mph, the push in the back is still strong and smooth. Not until 140 mph does the car's acceleration taper off. The 328 has as much shove at that speed as the old 308 (a carburetted version) has at 110, notwithstanding the older car's light weight and the good throttle response of the carburettor engine.'

The *Motor* report, which gave a 0–60 mph time of 5.5 sec, followed on by saying, 'the 328's overtaking punch in fourth and fifth gears is, if anything, even more impressive. Although the 32

Minor alterations to the interior of the Mondial mean red graphics for the instruments

valver feels a cammy unit on the road, its measured flexibility is astonishing. As if the 308 Qv's ability to put away all the 20 mph increments between 20 and 110 mph in around 5 seconds apiece in fourth gear wasn't enough, the 328 cuts the time taken to cover each increment to around 4.5 sec. Even in fifth, 80–100 mph takes a mere 7.9 sec.'

The increase in performance has apparently not been gained at the expense of fuel economy. In comparison with the older carburetted 308, which Cropley reckoned 'can manage 19 mph on a couple of hundred miles of Sunday morning sprinting', the 328 returns anything up to 23 mpg, and probably goes harder on the journey. Driven gently it can do 25 mpg. *Motor* were a shade more pessimistic with an overall consumption of 18.9 mpg but a projected touring consumption of 22.5 mpg.

To complete the range, 3.2-litre versions of the Mondial and Mondial Cabriolet are also available.

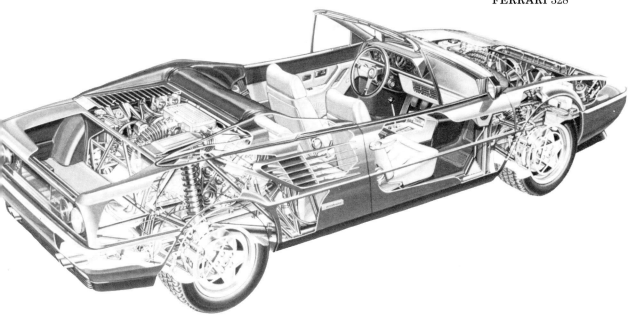

The front- and rear-end treatment given to both these models is clearly in line with that of the GTB/GTS cars in the series, insofar as lights, spoilers, etc, are concerned. Gone are the deep, black, wrap-round-to-the-wheel-wells bumpers that were a distinctive feature of previous Mondials. They have been replaced—and most feel for the better—by the combined bumper/underfairings that are deeper in appearance and colour matched to the rest of the car. It is a change that has greatly improved the look of the cars. Another change affects the wheels. While retaining the five-star design that has become almost a hallmark of Ferrari over the last decade, the star has been made convex and more pleasing to the eye. Wheel size at the front has gone down from 180 TR 390 to 165 TR 390, which has been done to lighten steering at low speeds and for parking. There are also some minor changes to the interiors, the most noticeable of which is the change to red graphics for the instruments.

Autocar in their issue of 25 June 1986 carried

Basically it is the same but better

127

The hood folds away under this rather ill-fitting cover

a road test report on a 3.2 Mondial. Compared to the Mondial 8, the figures for acceleration from 0–60 mph and 0–100 mph are now 6.8 and 16.5 respectively, the latter figure reflecting the additional strength in the mid-range performance that has been noted for the GTB/GTS cars. The 20 mph increment time in fourth gear is around 1.0 sec slower than that for the GTB/GTS, with the 80–100 mph time in fifth gear increased by 2.0 sec. These worthwhile increases in performance are, for the time being, keeping Ferrari's small 2+2 in the hunt. Its future, though, is not assured. By many accounts it is scheduled to be dropped from future production.

The 328s continue the process of broadening the appeal of Ferrari that started with the introduction of the V6-engined Dino 206/246 series and carried on through the V8-engined 308/Mondial range. It is a policy that has kept the name of the marque well to the fore of those constructors who specialize in the building of high-performance GT cars.

When the 308s were introduced, they were a significant departure from that which had gone before and there were many who hankered for a continuation of the past. Now, far enough removed from the early years, there is an appreciation that change was inevitable and that the 308/328 series has been instrumental in bringing it through at an acceptable rate.

What of the future? In many ways it remains as obscure as ever, though there is obviously no thought on the part of Ferrari to rest on their laurels. Rumours run thick and fast, but it seems that Ferrari have no intention of ditching the V8s nor of getting involved in turbocharging for the bulk of their road-going cars. From the straws now scattered on the wind it would appear that the best forecast, insofar as the V8s are concerned, is a continuation of gradual increases in engine capacity—there are strong indications that the next series of cars will have 3.4-litre engines.

More generally, *Cavallino* in their September/October 1986 issue may have given a clear indication of future trends when they noted: 'Enzo Ferrari recently said an intriguing thing. The customer of today doesn't necessarily want amazing top speed, although Ferrari will continue to supply that. What the customer really wants now, Mr Ferrari said, is instant speed, in other words, 0 to 60 and 0 to 100 mph by the fastest possible route. So while Ferraris will always top out at 160 mph, there will be a concerted effort to lower the 0 to 60 and 0 to 100 times to a minimum, all coupled with greater traction, better car control and better brakes. Look for six speed gearboxes, Torsen type differentials, four wheel drives with variable torque split, electronic suspensions, automatic ride heights and ABS brakes. All will be quite common by the end of the decade, and no doubt Ferrari will have high-tech versions of them all.'

The shape of things to come? Actually a styling exercise built on a Mondial floorplan for PPG Industries by IDEA of Turin as a pace car for the PPG/Indy Car Racing Series. Ferrari say it incorporates 'many new styling and mechanical concepts that could lead to a production model'

Type and chassis numbering

Ferrari type numbering for external use, as opposed to any internal system that may be in operation within the factory, is easy to understand because, for the majority of models made, one or the other of two simple systems has been used.

For the V12s and in-line four-cylinder-engined cars—with a handful of exceptions—the type number by which the cars are generally known is, in round figures, the displacement in cubic centimetres of one cylinder. From that, and knowing the number of cylinders, the capacity of the engine can be quickly derived; for example, a V12-engined Type 330GT will have a 4-litre engine, and a four-cylinder Type 750 Monza, a 3-litre engine.

The second system, introduced with the V6-engined cars and continued with the V8s—except for the Mondial series—uses a three figure number to designate the type. The first two figures give the overall displacement of the engine in litres and the third figure is the number of cylinders. The Dino 246 is therefore a 2.4-litre six-cylinder-engined car and a Dino 308 one with a 3-litre eight-cylinder engine.

Up until the introduction of the 3.2 Mondial, the Mondial series of cars with their adoption of a model name gave no clue to engine capacity. The name Mondial was not new to Ferrari, however, having been used back in the mid-1950s for a 2-litre in-line four-cylinder-engined sports car, the 500 Mondial.

To supplement type numbers, suffixes are used to give further indication of the type of car. With the 308 series those used are 'GT' Gran Turismo, 'S' Spider, 'B' Berlinetta and '4' to indicate the use of four camshafts, i.e. two per bank.

Chassis numbering—ignoring some complexities with the early cars and occasional contradictions amongst later models—is also straightforward. The competition cars—single seaters excepted—have even numbers, two apart, and the road cars have odd numbers, also two apart. An important departure has been the Dino series of cars—including the 308GT4s—which have been even numbered in their own sequence.

Withdrawal from works participation in sports car racing at the close of the 1973 season has kept the chassis numbers for the competition sports Ferraris below 1000, the last of the 312PBs in 1973 being numbered '0896'. The 365GTB/4 Daytonas and Boxers which have since appeared at Le Mans and other events are numbered in the sequence for the road cars on which they are based.

For the road cars—other than the Dino range—chassis numbers are now up into the early 70,000s, which indicates a total Ferrari production of some 35,000 cars since 1947, including the 328s—still in production—and the now completed 308GTS/GTB and Mondial 8/Mondial Qv series.

The last of the 308GT4s in the Dino series is said to be chassis '15604', which suggests a total production of some 7800 cars. Of these, the latest count suggests that 3883 were Dino 246s, leaving the balance to be distributed amongst the Dino 206 (150 made), the Italian market 208GT4 (some 800 made), and the 308GT4 (just under 3000 produced—a figure of 2826 has been given).

When this book was first published in 1982, it was noted that because the 308GTB/GTS and Mondial cars were numbered in the Ferrari odd-number system, it was not possible to employ simple arithmetic to arrive at numbers made; production of the models covered was still continuing and it was not the practice with Ferraris to allocate a batch of numbers to a particular model. They were numbered as they came through, irrespective of type or version. Since then, production of those cars has come to an end and figures have been released of numbers made. Where available, details are given in the following specifications.

To come up to date on chassis numbering, a piece of EEC legislation has resulted in the chassis number becoming part of a 17 digit sequence known as the 'Vehicle Identification Number' (VIN). A combination of letters and numbers, the VIN seeks to provide a unique identification for each car made by codifying information relating to the manufacturer, engine type, safety system (i.e. seat belt arrangement), model designation, destination, model year, place of manufacture and chassis number. So far, for Ferraris, the last five figures of the VIN are the chassis number.

Specifications

The 308GT4 has been taken as the base model, with principal variations noted only for the other models being dealt with. Also, because there can be market destination differences, the details given are generally those for the UK models but, at the level of information given, should be applicable to most of the cars sold within the continent of Europe.

308GT4

Introduced Paris Salon, autumn 1973. Production continued through into late 1980. Total production has been given as 2826.

Engine

Cylinders (number and arrangement)	8 in 90 degree Vee
Bore	81 mm (3.188 in.)
Stroke	71 mm (2.795 in.)
Cubic capacity	2926 cc (179 cid)
Cylinder block	Light aluminium alloy with removable cast-iron wet cylinder liners.
Cylinder heads	Light aluminium alloy with inserted cast-iron valve seats.
Number of valves per cylinder	Two
Valve operation	Twin overhead camshafts per bank. Toothed belt driven. Valves opened by bucket type tappets, closed by double helical coil springs. Clearance adjustment by shims.
Valve timing	Inlet open 34 deg btdc
	Inlet closes 46 deg abdc
	Exhaust opens 36 deg bbdc
	Exhaust closes 38 deg atdc
Lubrication system	Wet sump. Oil cooling radiator in engine compartment.
Cooling	Water. Radiator at front of car. Electric cooling fans.
Ignition	Battery and coils with twin or single distributors.
Firing order	1–5–3–7–4–8–2–6
Fuel system	Electric pump supplying from two tanks mounted in engine compartment to 4 double choke Weber Type 40 DCNF carburettors.
Maximum power	250 bhp at 7000 rpm
Maximum torque	29 kgm (209 lb ft) at 5000 rpm

Note: Figures for maximum power and torque are subject to variation according to the source quoted and from results achieved in practice with—particularly in the USA—varying degrees of anti-smog equipment. The figures quoted are typical of those given out for European version cars. For the USA a lowest figure of 205 bhp at 6600 rpm has been listed.

Transmission

Type	Manual. 5 forward speeds (full synchromesh) and reverse. Below and in unit with engine. Own oil supply. Step down gear train transfers drive from crankshaft to input shaft of constant mesh gearbox. Output through limited slip type differential to drive shafts with universal joints.
Clutch	Dry, single plate diaphragm type. Mechanically operated.

Gear ratios	1st gear	3.418
	2nd gear	2.353
	3rd gear	1.693
	4th gear	1.244
	5th gear	0.952
	Reverse	3.247 Final drive ratio 3.71:1
Steering		Rack and pinion type by Cam Gears. 3.28 turns lock to lock. Minimum turning circle 12 m. (39 ft).
Front suspension		Independent. Unequal length upper and lower A-arms, coil springs, Koni double acting hydraulic shock absorbers each side, anti-roll bar. Rubber bump and rebound stops.
Rear suspension		Independent. Unequal length upper and lower A-arms, coil springs, Koni double acting hydraulic shock absorbers each side, anti-roll bar. Rubber bump and rebound stops.
Brakes		Ventilated discs all round. Vacuum servo assisted. Tandem master cylinder arrangement linked to servo system. Pressure limiting valve in rear circuit. Mechanically operated parking/emergency brake on rear wheels.
Wheels		Light alloy type. 14 in. × 6½ in. Fitted with 205/70 VR 14 tubeless tyres. Also available 16 in. × 7 in.(front) 8 in. (rear) fitted with Pirelli P7 tyres. Spare wheel (European version) 3½B × 18 in. rim fitted with 105 R 18 tubeless tyre. Full size spare for USA version.
Chassis/Body		Chassis tubular steel type. Body, 2 + 2 designed by Bertone, built by Scaglietti. Material—steel.

Dimensions

Overall length	4300 mm	(169.29 in.)
Overall width	1710 mm	(67.32 in.)
Overall height	1210 mm	(47.63 in.)
Wheelbase	2550 mm	(100.39 in.)
Track – front	1460 mm	(57.87 in.)
– rear	1460 mm	(57.87 in.)
Dry weight	1365 kg	(3009 lb)
Chassis numbers	Possible range 07202 to 15604	

308GTB/GTBi/GTB Qv

308GTB introduced at Paris Salon, autumn 1975. Continued in production through the fuel-injected GTBi version, which became available early in 1981, and the four-valves-per-cylinder *quattrovalvole* Qv, which was introduced in the autumn of 1982. Total production of these models has been given as: 308GTB—2897; GTBi—494; GTB Qv—748.

GTB

	Specification generally as for 308GT4 but:
Valve timing	Inlet opens 30 deg btdc
	Inlet closes 50 deg abdc
	Exhaust opens 36 deg bbdc
	Exhaust closes 28 deg atdc
Maximum power	230 bhp at 7700 rpm (early publications gave 255 bhp at 7700 rpm)
Maximum torque	26.3 kgm (190 lb ft) at 4600 rpm (early publications gave 29 kgm, or 209 lb ft, at 5000 rpm)

Transmission	5th gear ratio 0.918
Lubrication system	Dry sump (except in USA where is wet sump)
Body	Designed by Pininfarina, built by Scaglietti. Material was initially fibreglass but reverted to steel during 1977 production.
Dimensions	
Overall length	4230 mm (166.5 in.) USA model 4378 mm (172.4 in.)
Overall width	1720 mm (67.71 in.)
Overall height	1120 mm (44.09 in.)
Wheelbase	2340 mm (92.12 in.)
Track front/rear	1460 mm (57.48 in.)
Dry weight	1265 kg (2788 lb)
Chassis numbers	Started 18677. Last fibreglass-bodied car 21289. First steel-bodied car 20805. Last rhd car 34347.

GTBi

Valve timing	Specification generally as for GTB but:
	Inlet opens 16 deg btdc
	Inlet closes 48 deg abdc
	Exhaust opens 54 deg bbdc
	Exhaust closes 10 deg atdc
Maximum power	214 bhp at 6600 rpm
Maximum torque	24.8 kgm (179 lb ft) at 4600 rpm
	Note: USA reports give maximum power as 205 bhp at 6600 rpm and maximum torque as 181 lb ft at 5000 rpm.
Tyres	240/55 VR 390 Michelin TRX
Lubrication system	Wet sump for all versions
Fuel system	Weber carburettors replaced by Bosch K Jetronic fuel injection
Final drive ratio	4.06
Ignition	Electronic by Marelli Digiplex
Chassis numbers	Started 31327. Last rhd car 42617.

GTB Qv

	Specification generally as for GTB/GTBi models but: Revised cylinder head incorporating four valves per cylinder
Maximum power	240 bhp at 7000 rpm
Maximum torque	26.5 kgm (191 lb ft) at 5000 rpm
	Note: USA reports gave maximum power as 230 bhp at 6800 rpm and maximum torque as 188 lb ft at 5500 rpm.
Wheels	165 TR 390 front and rear, with Michelin TRX 225/55 VR 390 tyres. Optional wheel sizes 7J × 16 front and 8J × 16 rear, with Pirelli P7 205/55 VR 16 and 225/50 VR 16 tyres respectively.
Final drive ratio	3.82
Chassis numbers	First rhd car 43247. Last rhd car 58255.

308GTS/GTSi/GTS Qv

308GTS introduced at Frankfurt Salon, autumn 1977. Continued in production through the fuel-injected GTSi version, which became available early in 1981, and the four-valves-per-cylinder *quattrovalvole* Qv version, which was introduced in the autumn of 1982. Production of this 308 series ceased in 1985 following the introduction of the 328 series. Total numbers made are said to be: 308GTS—3219; GTSi—1743; GTS Qv—3042.

GTS

	Specification generally as for GTB but body made of steel throughout production and engine lubrication by wet sump for all destinations.
Chassis numbers	Started at 22619. Last rhd car 32407.

GTSi

	Specification generally as for GTBi.
Chassis numbers	Started at 31309. Last rhd car 42617.

GTS Qv

	Specification generally as for GTB Qv.
Chassis numbers	First rhd car 43147. Last rhd car 58751.

Mondial 8/Mondial Qv/Mondial Cabriolet

The Mondial 8 was introduced at the Geneva Show, March 1980. A Qv version became available in August 1982, and the Cabriolet model introduced in America in October 1983 was first shown in Europe at the 1984 Brussels Motor Show. Total production of these models has been given as: Mondial 8—703; Mondial Qv—1144; Mondial Cabriolet—629.

Mondial 8

Valve timing	Specification generally as for 308GT4 but:
	Inlet opens 16 deg btdc
	Inlet closes 48 deg abdc
	Exhaust opens 54 deg bbdc
	Exhaust closes 10 deg atdc
Ignition	Electronic by Marelli Digiplex
Fuel system	Electric pump supplying from two tanks mounted under rear seats to fuel accumulator of Bosch K Jetronic fuel injection

Maximum power	214 bhp at 6600 rpm (USA version 205 bhp at 6600 rpm)
Maximum torque	179 lb ft at 4600 rpm (USA version 181 lb ft at 5000 rpm)
Transmission	5th gear ratio 0.919. Final drive ratio 4.06. Clutch—dry, single plate diaphragm type, hydraulically operated.
Wheels	Light alloy 180 TR 390
Tyres	240/55 VR 390 Michelin TRX
Chassis	Arranged so that engine, transaxle and rear suspension may be extracted as a unit for servicing.
Body	Designed by Pininfarina, built by Scaglietti. Material, steel.
Dimensions	
Overall length	4580 mm (180.3 in.)
Overall width	1790 mm (70.5 in.)
Overall height	1250 mm (49.2 in.)
Wheelbase	2650 mm (104.3 in.)
Track—front	1495 mm (58.9 in.)
—rear	1517 mm (59.7 in.)
Curb Weight	1445 kg (3179 lb)
Chassis numbers	Started at 31075. Last rhd car 41359.

Mondial Qv

	Specification generally as for Mondial 8 but: Revised cylinder head incorporating four valves per cylinder
Maximum power	240 bhp at 7700 rpm
Maximum torque	26.5 kgm (191 lb ft) at 5000 rpm
	Note: For USA version, figures are 230 bhp at 7700 rpm and 26 kgm at 5500 rpm.
Chassis numbers	First rhd car 42955. Last rhd car 58619.

Mondial Cabriolet

	Specification as for Mondial Qv.
Chassis numbers	First rhd car 50513. Last rhd car 58913.

328GTB/GTS/3.2 Mondial/3.2 Mondial Cabriolet

All introduced at the 1985 Frankfurt Show. Production continues, though it was reported that the following numbers were produced during 1986: 328GTB—372; 328GTS—1483; 3.2 Mondial and 3.2 Mondial Cabriolet—564. In terms of general specification, all are closely related to the previous 308 or Mondial series cars.

328GTB/GTS

	Specification generally as for 308GTB Qv/GTS Qv but:
Bore	83 mm
Stroke	73.6 mm
Cubic capacity	3185 cc
Maximum power	270 bhp at 7000 rpm (USA—260 bhp at 7000 rpm)
Maximum torque	31 kgm (223 lb ft) at 5500 rpm (USA—28.6 kgm, or 213 lb ft, at 5500 rpm)
Compression ratio	9.2:1 (USA—9.8:1)
Ignition	Marelli Microplex
Dimensions	
Overall length	4255 mm (167.5 in.)
Overall width	1730 mm (68.1 in.)
Overall height	1128 mm (44.4 in.)
Wheelbase	2350 mm (92.5 in.)
Track—front	1485 mm (58.4 in.)
—rear	1465 mm (57.7 in.)
Final drive ratio	3.7:1
Wheels	7J × 16 front and 8J × 16 rear
Tyres	Goodyear 205/55 VR 16 and Goodyear 225/50 VR 16 respectively. Pirelli P7s listed as optional in the same sizes.
Chassis numbers	First rhd cars 60841 (GTB) and 60765 (GTS).

3.2 Mondial/3.2 Mondial Cabriolet

	Specification generally as for Mondial and Mondial Cabriolet but:
Bore	83 mm
Stroke	73.6 mm
Cubic capacity	3185 cc
Maximum power	270 bhp at 7000 rpm (USA—260 bhp at 7000 rpm)
Maximum torque	31 kgm (223 lb ft) at 5500 rpm (USA—28.6 kgm, or 213 lb ft, at 5500 rpm)
Compression ratio	9.8:1 (USA—9.2:1)
Ignition	Marelli Microplex
Dimensions	
Overall length	4535 mm (178.5 in.)
Track—front	1473 mm (58 in.) (USA—1520 mm/59.8 in.)
—rear	1468 mm (57.8 in.) (USA—1510 mm/59.4 in.)
Chassis numbers	First rhd cars 61047 (3.2 Mondial) and 62561 (3.2 Mondial Cabriolet).

Additional reading

The 308 and Mondial Ferraris have been the subject of very many write-ups and road test reports in the motoring press—presumably the 328s and 3.2 Mondials will follow suit. The list which follows is by no means exhaustive, covering as it does only English language articles and not all of those. It should, however, provide the reader with a useful reference to the more readily available material. Some of the journals in which articles originally appeared may no longer be available in which case the 'Brooklands Books' series on Ferraris can often help with their reprints of articles. For the 308 series their *Ferrari Cars 1973–1977, Ferrari Cars 1977–1981* and *Ferrari 308 and Mondial 1980–1984* are the most useful, and the repeat of an article in these is covered by the entry 'BB 73/77' etc in the list. More recent titles in the series cover specifically Ferrari articles which

have appeared in the American magazine *Road & Track* during the years 1968–1974 and 1975–1981. All the *Road & Track* articles listed are covered by these latest Brooklands Books.

In the list the terms 'Impressions' and 'Full R/T report' may need a little bit of explanation. The 'Impressions' articles generally contain only limited specification and test data. They are based upon road driving experience of the cars in question, sometimes for only a very short distance but mostly for many hundreds of miles, and for the most part are very informative, particularly—if one may make a personal choice—those that have appeared in *Car* magazine. The 'Full R/T report' contains descriptive material supplemented to varying degrees by specification and performance test data.

308GT4
1	*Motor*	UK	25.5.79	Impressions + accl. data	
2	*Autocar*	UK	28.9.74	Design analysis	
3	*Road & Track*	USA	Sep. 74	Impressions + general data and accl. figures. USA version of 1	BB 73/77
4	*Motor Sport*	UK	Oct. 74	Impressions + data in text	BB 73/77
5	*Car*	UK	Nov. 74	Impressions + accl. data	
6	*Autosport*	UK	12.12.74	R/T report. General data + accl.	
7	*Motor*	UK	11.1.75	Full R/T report	
8	*Autocar*	UK	16.8.75	Comparison with Dino 246GT	BB 73/77
9	*Road & Track*	USA	Sep. 75	Comparison with Maserati Merak and Lamborghini Urraco P111	
10	*Car*	UK	Oct. 75	Impressions by another writer to 5 above	
11	*Road Test*	USA	Mar. 76	Full R/T report and Tech Scan	BB 73/77
12	*Autocar*	UK	13.3.76	Full R/T report	BB 73/77
13	*Road & Track*	USA	Nov. 79	Late in life R/T report	

308 GTB
14	*Motor*	UK	29.11.75	Impressions + accl. data	
15	*Car*	UK	July 76	Impressions	BB 73/77
16	*Autosport*	UK	29.7.76	R/T report. General data + accl.	
17	*Motor*	UK	11.9.76	Impressions also general data and accl.	
18	*Autocar*	UK	23.10.76	Full R/T report	
19	*Motor Sport*	UK	Dec. 76	Impressions	BB 73/77
20	*Road & Track*	USA	Dec. 76	Track impressions by Bob Bondurant	BB 73/77
21	*Road & Track*	USA	Feb. 77	Full R/T report	
22	*Modern Motor*	AUS	July 77	Full R/T report	BB 73/77
23	*Autocar*	UK	15.4.78	Impressions of 308GTB fitted with Pirelli P7 tyres	
24	*Car*	UK	Oct. 78	Impressions. Comparison with Maserati Merak SS and Lamborghini Urraco P300	

308GTBi
25	*Car*	UK	June 81	Back-to-back test with Lotus Turbo Esprit	BB 77/81
26	*Motor Sport*	UK	Mar. 83	Impressions	BB 80/84
27	*Car & Driver*	USA	Aug. 83	Full R/T report	BB 80/84
28	*Motor*	UK	29.10.83	Full R/T report	BB 80/84

308GTS
29	*Road & Track*	USA	July 76	Full R/T report	
30	*Motor*	UK	26.8.78	Impressions. Comparison with Porsche 911 SC Targa. General data and accl.	
31	*Car & Driver*	USA	June 78	Full R/T report	

308GTSi
32	*Road & Track*	USA	Mar. 81	Full R/T report	

Mondial 8
33	*Autocar*	UK	24.4.80	General description	BB 77/81
34	*Car*	UK	July 81	Impressions	
35	*Motor Sport*	UK	Aug. 81	Impressions	
36	*Road & Track*	USA	Nov. 81	Full R/T report	
37	*Motor Trend*	USA	Nov. 81	Full R/T report	
38	*Car & Driver*	USA	Nov. 81	Full R/T report. Some comparison data with Porsche 928 and Jaguar XJ-S	
39	*Motor*	UK	5.12.81	Impressions	

ADDITIONAL READING

Mondial Qv

40	*Motor*	UK	30.10.82	Full R/T report	BB 80/84

Mondial Cabriolet

41	*Road & Track*	USA	May 84	Full R/T report	BB 80/84

328GTB

42	*Motor*	UK	21.6.86	Full R/T report
43	*Autocar*	UK	17.6.87	Full R/T report

3.2 Mondial

44	*Autocar*	UK	25.6.86	Full R/T report

Special

45	*Road & Track*	USA	Aug. 77	Rainbow. Impression of Bertone's 1976 Turin Salon car based on 308GT4 chassis	BB 73/77
46	*Car*	UK	Feb. 78	Rainbow alongside Bertone's Jaguar XJ-S based Ascot	
47	*Car*	UK	Oct. 81	Impressions of Janspeed Engineering-prepared turbocharged 308GTB	
48	*Car*	UK	July 81	Visit to factory. Good background article to modern range of Ferrari	

The following chassis numbers are associated with rhd cars built from 1974 onwards. The numbers are those of the first car in each of the years listed, together with some additional numbers at points where a more noticeable change of specification/option has taken place.

Model	Year	Chassis No.		Remarks
308GT4	1974	08354	May 74	Basic specification. Electric windows, tinted glass and heated rear window, standard
	1975	08918	Jan. 75	Electric windows, tinted glass and heated rear window, extra
	1976	11800	Jan. 76	Continued
		12288	May 76	Revised grille with 3 horizontal and 6 vertical strips. Ferrari motifs on bonnet, road wheels and steering wheel. Improved air conditioning with added outlets beneath instrument panel
		12722	Oct. 76	Electric windows, tinted glass and heated rear window, standard
	1977	13120	Jan. 77	Continued
	1978	13986	Jan. 78	Continued
	1979	14500	Jan. 79	Continued
	1980	15402	Jan. 80	Continued
		15474	Dec. 80	Discontinued. Final chassis number
308GTB	1976	19149	May 76	Basic specification
	1977	20503	Jan. 77	Continued
		21253	May 77	Last fibreglass-bodied version
		21333	May 77	First steel-bodied version
		22513	Dec. 77	Big front spoiler optional extra. No spare wheel cover
	1978	23207	Jan. 78	Continued
	1979	26639	Jan. 79	Continued
		27261	June 79	Recessed clock, oil and temperature gauges
		28393	July 79	Gas struts on rear lid
	1980	30379	Jan. 80	Continued
	1981	34347	Mar. 81	Last GTB version. Replaced by GTBi.
308GTBi	1981	35257	Mar. 81	Bosch K Jetronic fuel injection. Interior trim changed
	1982	40031	Jan. 82	Continued
308GTB Qv	1982	43247	Oct. 82	Quattrovalvole version introduced. Replaced GTBi
	1983	44649	Jan. 83	Continued
	1984	48759	Jan. 84	Continued
	1985	55375	Jan. 85	Continued
		58255	Aug. 85	Quattrovalvole discontinued. Replaced by 328GTB
328GTB	1986	60841	Jan. 86	Introduced Oct. 85, available Jan. 86. Body similar to 308GTB, but with grille now enclosing rectangular light units incorporating fog, side and flasher units set in moulded bumper. High rear aerofoil optional
	1987	68375	Jan. 87	Continued
		73059	July 87	Interior door handles changed
308GTS	1978	23419	Feb. 78	Spider version of GTB. First cars imported had detachable section in roof
	1979	26635	Jan. 79	Continued
		28393	Jun/July 79	Modified as 308GTB. See above
	1980	30119	Jan. 80	Continued
	1981	32047	Mar. 81	Last GTS version. Replaced by GTSi
308GTSi	1981	34995	Mar. 81	Bosch K Jetronic fuel injection. Interior trim changed
	1982	40171	Jan. 82	Continued
308GTS Qv	1982	43147	Oct. 82	Quattrovalvole version introduced. Replaced GTSi
	1983	44437	Jan. 83	Continued
		47341	Sep. 83	Continued but with colour-keyed windscreen surround
	1984	48799	Jan. 84	Continued
	1985	55187	Jan. 85	Continued
		58751	Aug. 85	Discontinued. Replaced by 328GTS
328GTS	1986	60765	Jan. 86	Introduced Oct. 85, available Jan. 86. Styling details as for 328GTB
	1987	67837	Jan. 87	Continued
		73021	July 87	Interior door handles changed
Mondial 8	1981	33737	Aug. 81	Introduced. 2 + 2 coupé body. Digiplex electronic ignition and Bosch K Jetronic fuel injection. Leather upholstery standard. Digital displays, air conditioning standard. Electric windows, central locking
	1982	39137	Jan. 82	Continued
Mondial Qv	1982	42955	Aug. 82	Quattrovalvole version introduced. Replaced Mondial 8
	1983	44363	Jan. 83	Continued
		46521	Jun. 83	Minor interior changes, e.g. box with lid replaced soft pocket between seats. Cabriolet version introduced into USA in September
	1984	48873	Jan. 84	Continuation of Qv version
		50513	Jun. 84	Cabriolet version introduced
	1985	55207	Jan. 85	Qv 2 + 2 version continued
		53355	Jan. 85	Cabriolet version continued
		58619	Sep. 85	Qv 2 + 2 version discontinued. Replaced by 3.2 Mondial
		58913	Sep. 85	Cabriolet version discontinued. Replaced by 3.2 Cabriolet
3.2 Mondial	1986	61047 } 62561	Jan. 86	2 + 2 and Cabriolet versions introduced Oct. 85, available Jan. 86. Styling generally similar to 328GTB/GTS. Rear wings house radiator grilles. Circular rear light clusters
	1987	67973 } 68847	Jan. 87	2 + 2 and Cabriolet versions continued

Acknowledgements

As more and more books are being published on the subject of Ferrari it becomes more and more difficult to illustrate any such book. It means a constant search for new sources—a successful result is shown here, we trust—however, many of the stalwarts are still there unearthing fresh material.

Five major sources produced illustrations and information; we are grateful to all, of course—SEFAC Ferrari at the Maranello press office, Pininfarina Industrie SpA in Turin, Mark Konig of Maranello Sales, Ivan Bishop of Graypaul Motors Ltd, and Janspeed Engineering Ltd.

Considerable assistance was given to researcher Mirco Decet by Godfrey Eaton of the UK-based Ferrari Owners Club, by Ferrari enthusiasts Jonathan Thompson and Jean-Francois Marchet. Others' contributions were by no means make-weights either.

They were the late Peter Coltrin, Gene Babon, Andrew Bell, John Lamm, Geoff Goddard, Alessandro Stefanini, Anthony Corlett, Image Public Relations, Hunziker and Tim Parker Collection.

Special thanks must go to June Willoughby and John Aley.

Index